Teach Yourself Accents
Europe

Teach Yourself Accents Europe

A Handbook for Young Actors and Speakers

Robert Blumenfeld

An Imprint of Hal Leonard Corporation

Published in 2014 by Limelight Editions
An Imprint of Hal Leonard Corporation
7777 West Bluemound Road
Milwaukee, WI 53213

Trade Book Division Editorial Offices
33 Plymouth St., Montclair, NJ 07042

Printed in the United States of America

Book design by Mark Lerner

Library of Congress Cataloging-in-Publication Data

Blumenfeld, Robert.
 Teach yourself accents : Europe : a handbook for young actors and speakers / Robert Blumenfeld.
     pages cm
 Includes bibliographical references.
 ISBN 978-0-87910-809-0
 1. Acting. 2. English language--Pronunciation by foreign speakers.
 3. English language--Dialects--Europe--Handbooks, manuals, etc. I. Title.
 PN2071.F6B482 2014
 792.02'8--dc23
                              2013050072

www.limelighteditions.com

With gratitude and inexpressible love to my wonderful,
sweet, brilliant parents, Max David Blumenfeld (1911–1994)
and Ruth Blumenfeld (b. 1915)

CONTENTS

ACKNOWLEDGMENTS

I would like to thank my many language teachers at Princeton High School and at Rutgers and Columbia Universities. I extend thanks, also, to the staff of the Stella Adler Conservatory; to Mr. Albert Schoemann, Ms. Pamela Hare, and Mr. Mark Zeller at the once-flourishing National Shakespeare Conservatory; and to my students at both of these schools. Very special thanks are due to my wonderful friend Mr. Christopher Buck for his love and support, always. I want to express my thanks and gratitude to my friend Mr. Derek Tague for his special contribution in lending me rare books on accents. I would also like to thank my very dear and beloved friends for their unfailing support and love over the many years we have known one another: Albert S. Bennett; Marvin Starkman; Tom and Virginia Smith; Peter Subers and Rob Bauer; Kieran Mulcare and Daniel Vosovic; Michael Mendiola and Scot Anderson; and my family: Nina Koenigsberg, my cousins' cousin; my brother Donald Blumenfeld-Jones, my sister-in-law Kathryn Corbeau Blumenfeld-Jones and their children, Rebecca and Benjamin; my maternal aunt Mrs. Bertha Friedman (1913–2001) and her daughter, my cousin Marjorie Loewer; my maternal uncle Seymour "Sy" Korn (1920–2010); my paternal cousin Jonathan Blumenfeld; and my wonderful maternal grandparents from the province of Galicia in the Austro-Hungarian Empire, Morris Korn (1886–1979) and Harriet Korn (1886–1980).

I especially want to thank Lon Davis, whose wonderful copy editing of my manuscript has been invaluable; Mark Lerner for his beautiful design; my editor, Ms. Jessica Burr, for her dedication and hard work; and my publisher and friend, Mr. John Cerullo, always forthright and encouraging. Special thanks are due to Mr. Mel Zerman (1931–2010), founder and publisher of Limelight Editions, who was not only very helpful throughout the process of getting my first book, *Accents: A Manual for Actors*, published by Limelight in 1998, but was also a kind, charming, and erudite man, one who is greatly missed. I owe a great debt to the authors of the books listed in the Selected Bibliography, without whose work this book would have been impossible. All translations from French, German, Italian, Russian, Spanish, Swedish, and Yiddish are my own.

LIST OF PHONETIC SYMBOLS USED IN THIS BOOK

Vowels and Semi-Vowels

ah: like "a" in *father*

a: like "a" in *that*

aw: like "aw" in *law*

ee: like "ee" in *meet*

e: like "e" in *met*

é: a pure vowel similar to the English diphthong "ay"; heard in French; lips close together

è: a pure vowel similar to the "e" in *met*, but more open; heard in French

ih: like "i" in *bit*

ih: a vowel intermediate between /ih/ and /ee/, pronounced with the mouth closed more than for /ih/ and open wider than for /ee/; used in many European accents in English, where /ih/ does not exist

o: like "o" in *not*

o: like "o" in *work*

oo: like "oo" in *book*; spelled "u" in *pull*

ooh: like "oo" in *boot*

u: like "u" in *but*

ü: the German umlauted "u" and the French vowel spelled "u" in French; pronounced by saying /ee/ with the lips well protruded, as for /ooh/; heard in some Scottish pronunciations uh: the schwa; the sound of "e" in *the* before a consonant: *the story*

y: the semi-vowel spelled "y" in *yes*

w: the semi-vowel spelled "w" in *wear* and *we* and "o" in *one*

Diphthongs

ay: the diphthong composed of /e/, which is the stressed half of the diphthong, and /ee/; spelled "ay" in *say*

I: the diphthong composed of /ah/, which is the stressed half of the diphthong, and /ee/; spelled "i" in *fight*

oh: the diphthong composed of /u/, which is the stressed half of the diphthong, and /ooh/ in American English; of the schwa /uh/ and /ooh/ in
British English; spelled "o" in *home*

ow: the diphthong composed of /a/, which is the stressed half of the diphthong, and /ooh/; spelled "ow" in *how* and "ou" in *house*

oy: the diphthong composed of /aw/, which is the stressed half of the
diphthong, and /ee/; spelled "oy" in *boy*

yooh: the diphthong composed of the semi-vowel /y/ and the vowel /ooh/,
which is the stressed half of the diphthong; spelled *you*. This diphthong
is the name of the letter "u" in the English alphabet.

Consonants

The consonants /b/, /d/, /f/, /g/ as in *get*, /k/, /h/, /l/, /m/, /n/, /p/, /r/, /s/,
/t/, /v/, and /z/ have the standard phonetic values of General American
English or British RP. The following additional symbols are used:

ch: like "ch" in *church*; a combination of the sounds /t/ and /sh/

j: like "dg" in *edge* or "j" in *just*

kh: like "ch" in Scottish *loch*; a guttural consonant in Arabic, Hebrew, Yiddish, and German

ng: like "ng" in *thing*

nk: like "nk" in *think*

[r]: r-influenced; appears after vowels that are r-influenced

sh: like "sh" in *show*

th: voiced, as in *this*

th: voiceless, as in *thing*

ts: like "ts" in *sets*

zh: like "s" in *measure, pleasure*

?: glottal stop, which replaces the sound of /t/ in certain words in some accents

Pronunciations are enclosed in forward slash marks: / /.

Tones in intonation patterns in chapter 3 on German accents, chapter 7 on Swedish accents, and chapter 8 on Yiddish accents:

A forward slash indicates a rising tone: /.

A backward slash indicates a single falling tone; also, Accent One in Swedish: \.

Two backward slashes indicate a compound falling tone, Accent Two in Swedish: \\.

Stressed syllables in pronunciations are in capital letters.

Teach Yourself Accents: The Elements

What Is an Accent?

An accent is a systematic pattern of pronunciation: the prototypical, in-separable combination of sounds, rhythm, and intonation with which a language is spoken. Nearly everyone who grows up in a specific region and social milieu pronounces the language in a similar way, so we can usually tell from someone's accent where that person is from, and to what socio-economic class an individual belongs.

In show business, we use the words *accent* and *dialect* interchangeably, as in the title "dialect coach" for someone who teaches accents to actors, but, technically, they are not the same thing. A dialect is a complete ver-sion or variety of a language, with its grammar and vocabulary, as well as the particular accent or accents with which it is spoken.

Like every language, English has its dialects, including those known as Standard British English and Standard American English. Although mutually comprehensible, these dialects are dissimilar in many ways: An English person is "meant" to do something; an American is "supposed" to do it. In London, people live in flats; in New York, they live in apartments. An English person who wants to visit you may "knock you up," but don't say that to an American! As George Bernard Shaw quipped, "England and America are two countries separated by a common language." Then there are Standard Scottish English (SSE), Australian English (AusE), and many other varieties, each with its own accents, idioms, and colorful slang. In Sydney, if you're thirsty, you might want to whip over on the knocker (immediately) to the bottle-shop (liquor store) for some cold tinnies of amber (beer). But in Glasgow you would go to an *offie*, a shortening of the U.K. term "off license," a store where you buy alcoholic beverages to be consumed off the premises. Go get a carry-out before the offie shuts!

There are two kinds of accents: those native to a language, and foreign accents, used by people with a different mother tongue who have learned a language. The two principal standard native accents of English—markedly different from each other—are known as British RP ("Received Pronunciation"), the accent with which Standard British English is spoken; and General American, the most widely used accent of Standard American English.

The muscular habits you have learned automatically and unconsciously—the way you form and utter sounds using the lips, tongue, and resonating chamber that is the inside of the mouth—are so ingrained that it is often difficult to learn the new muscular habits required when you learn another language. Sounds that are similar in the new language to the sounds you already know are, therefore, formed using the old habits. And there are always sounds in the new language that do not exist in the old, and that some people have great difficulty learning to pronounce correctly, such as the /th / *th*/ sounds of English. These are two of the factors that account for the existence of a foreign accent, easily heard as foreign by native speakers. There are also people who learn to speak English or any other language with virtually no discernible foreign accent.

If you are going to do a foreign accent, it's essential to learn some of the language. You will then have a feeling for the muscular habits, for how the lips and tongue are positioned and used during speech. And you will use this basic positioning or placement of the muscles when speaking English. This will automatically give you at least the beginning of the accent. Sometimes this general positioning is all that is required, perhaps with a couple of specific vowel or consonant sounds added to it.

Native accents include a widely accepted, standard, non-regional accent alongside regional pronunciations. You unconsciously learn your accent from the people you go to school with and who surround you, even more than you do from your parents. If your parents speak with a foreign accent, for instance, you will nevertheless speak with the native accent that you hear constantly, at least if you have been born in a place, or arrived there when you were not yet twelve.

Accents, like languages, disappear when the last speaker dies. There are now only a relatively few upper-class Americans who speak as President Franklin D. Roosevelt did in 1941. The British accents recorded on Edison's wax cylinders by Florence Nightingale; by the poet Alfred, Lord Tennyson; and by actors of the late Victorian period, performing the works of Gilbert and Sullivan, no longer exist. And the native New York City accents of the 1920s and 1930s, preserved in films of the period, such as *Dead End* (1937), are largely a thing of the past, though still well remembered, but the American stage diction of the late nineteenth century as recorded by Edwin Booth in 1890 is something nobody now recalls, and it is different from the recorded British stage diction of the same period. Should you need to use one of these historic accents, you have ample recorded material to listen to.

Whether foreign or native, every accent contains four elements, each of which can be studied separately, but all of which work together simultaneously to form the accent:

1. General positioning, placement, and use of the mouth muscles (lips, tongue) during speech;
2. Rhythm, determined by stress patterns;
3. Music, determined by pitch and intonation patterns;
4. Phonetics, the specific sounds of vowels and consonants, the nature of those sounds being conditioned by the positioning of the mouth muscles, which differs—however slightly—from accent to accent.

Begin your work by reading the summary of the most important information about the accent, and by seeing how it differs from yours, comparing its features with those of your own accent. How do you naturally speak? How do you use the muscles of the mouth when you speak? How does this use differ when you do an accent?

Your goal as an actor is to internalize and assimilate the accent so that it becomes your natural, habitual way of speaking, so that it is simply part of you, and not put on. The one exception is when the character is deliberately pretending to be someone with an accent, often a bad, comical one that they intend to be convincing, like several Viennese characters posing as either French or Hungarian aristocrats in Johann Strauss's operetta *Die Fledermaus* (The Bat).

How the Muscles of the Mouth Are Used

The first thing to study when learning an accent is the way the muscles of the mouth are used when you speak. The musculature of the vocal apparatus is used in a different way in every language or accent; and a priori in a different way from what you are accustomed to in your own accent when you are learning a new one. There are, perhaps, only a few such basic placements or positions, but they condition the way vowels and consonants sound, and give each accent its own particular resonance and linguistic flavor.

To create an authentic-sounding light native or foreign accent it is sometimes sufficient to have the vocal apparatus positioned as it would be by someone who really speaks with that accent. The accent may then be thickened by adding certain phonetic changes. The general position of the vocal apparatus during speech is determined by four things: the place of articulation of the consonants (see later in this introduction); the positioning of the tongue when forming vowels; how much the lips are protruded; and how tight or loose the muscles are at the corners of the mouth.

Rhythm: Stress Patterns

Rhythm is created by the stress patterns of an accent. Stress indicates which syllables in a word are emphasized or are most prominent. Stressed syllables are usually longer (and louder, and spoken on a pitch differentiating them from adjacent pitches) than the shorter unstressed syllables, just as a half note is longer than a quarter note.

In English every word has its own particular unvarying primary stress, and there is secondary stressing in longer words. However, in British RP and General American, words may be stressed differently. An example is the word *controversy*: in British RP it is pronounced /kuhn TRO vuh see/; in General American, /KAHN truh VOR see/. Unless you have grown up speaking English, and thus learned English stress patterns automatically and unconsciously, you have to make an effort to learn the stress for every word. Stress in English is called "random": words could be stressed on any syllable, and you don't know where the stress is unless you have learned it.

In English, whichever word is stressed is the one that gives a sentence its meaning, not to be understood out of context. Take, for instance, the sentence "I never said he stole my money." Stressing a different word changes the meaning of the sentence; each meaning in parentheses indicates only one of several possibilities:

1. *I* never said he stole my money. (Maybe somebody else said it.)
2. I *never* said he stole my money. (You made that up!)
3. I never *said* he stole my money. (That doesn't mean I didn't think it.)
4. I never said *he* stole my money. (I said somebody else stole it.)
5. I never said he *stole* my money. (I gave it to him.)
6. I never said he stole *my* money. (It belonged to somebody else.)
7. I never said he stole my *money*. (He stole my keys.)

There are languages in which the first syllable of every word is always stressed, and other languages in which stress is always on the last syllable.

Languages in which a particular syllable is always stressed are said to have "uniform" stress. You always know how to stress words correctly even if you have no idea what they mean. This information is very important in creating a foreign accent, as such automatic habits can carry over into English.

The rhythmic stress patterns of a native language are often difficult to break, as they are so ingrained. They tend to carry over into English, although the correct random English stress patterns can be and often are learned. But the French accent, with its tendency to stress the last syllables of phrases, and the Hungarian accent, with its tendency to stress the first syllables of words, show how difficult it is to unlearn habits related to linguistic stress patterns.

Music: Intonation Patterns

Every accent has its own characteristic music, which is made up of a series of pitch or intonation patterns. Intonation means the pattern of pitch changes in connected speech—that is, in a sentence, phrase, or general utterance. All languages communicate by using a combination of pitch and stress, and the pitch and stress patterns are different in different languages. When you learn an accent, you must study these patterns along with the accent's phonetic aspects.

The pitch patterns (intonation patterns) in English express and convey emotion and meaning in ways we have automatically learned. We can choose to emphasize any word by saying it on a different pitch, higher or lower, from the surrounding pitches.

It is very difficult to describe the intonation patterns of any language, but every language has a distinctive intonation pattern, or systematic way of using pitches to express emotion. You simply have to hear them, and to learn what they mean.

Phonetics

You will make the actual sounds of an accent by learning how to do them physically. First, ask yourself how you make the vowel and consonant sounds of your own natural accent. Close your eyes and observe how those sounds "feel" in the mouth, and where they are placed. You can compare them to the new sounds of the accent. If you are an American doing a British RP accent, for instance, the sounds will feel more forward in the mouth than they do in your own accent, and the consonants will be more strongly articulated; that is, whatever muscle or part of the mouth presses against another part—the two lips, for instance, when saying /b/ or /p/—will be stronger in an upper-class British accent than in a General American accent.

Vowels, Semi-Vowels, and Diphthongs

A *vowel* is a single sound made by passing air through the vibrating vocal cords and then through the vocal cavity without the flow of air being stopped. The shape of the vocal cavity changes with each vowel; the tongue is higher or lower, the vocal cavity is more open or more closed, and the lips are relaxed or protruded or retracted, rounded or unrounded. The stream of air is directed up and either primarily to the back or middle or front of the palate (the "sounding board" of the mouth), and this is called the focal point, or what I mean by the point of resonance. Hence we refer, as I have said, to back and front vowels, which can be open or closed, rounded or unrounded. The vowel /ah/ in *father*, for example, is an open back unrounded vowel. There are also, as in French and Portuguese, nasal vowels, pronounced by lowering the soft palate at the back of the mouth and allowing some air to flow through the nasal cavity just above it, as when articulating the consonants /m/ and /n/.

A *semi-vowel* is a vowel during the pronunciation of which the flow of air is beginning to be stopped by the action of tongue or lips. It therefore has almost a consonantal quality. The two semi-vowels in English are /w/, during which the lips are beginning to close and are slightly rounded, and /y/, during which the sides of the tongue move up toward the roof of the mouth, touching it very lightly. They can interchangeably be called either semi-consonants or semi-vowels. Both /y/ and /w/ combine with vowels to form diphthongs: /yah/, /ye/, /yee/, /yoh/, /yoo/, /wah/, /we/, /wee/, /woh/, /woo/.

A *diphthong* consists of two vowels, or a vowel and a semi-vowel spoken in one breath. One of the vowels is always stressed. The unstressed half of the diphthong is always very short. An example is /I/, a combination of the /ah/ in *father* and the /ee/ in *meet*; /ah/ is stressed. In the case of diphthongs formed from a semi-vowel and a vowel, the vowel is always stressed: an example is the name of the letter "u" or the word *you*, formed with the semi-vowel /y/ and the vowel /ooh/ as in the word *boot*: /yOOH/. A diphthong occurs when the jaw relaxes slightly immediately after the pronunciation of a vowel and while sound is still issuing from the vocal cords. The tongue "glides" to a different position, changing the shape of the interior of the mouth, and we hear a diphthong.

Consonants

A *consonant* is a sound in which the flow of air is impeded or hindered by the action of tongue, lips, or teeth. Each consonant has a "point, or place, of articulation." The word *articulation* means how parts of the vocal apparatus touch each other to form a sound. For instance, to form a /t/, the tongue touches the palate (the roof of the mouth) just where it starts to curve upward, behind the front teeth—that is its point of articulation. The tongue may apply more or less pressure, and this changes the quality of the sound, making the /t/ hard or soft. In British RP, the /t/ is hard, as it is in the phrase *a cup of tea*. In General American, the /t/ is soft; that is, the pressure made by the tongue is not very strong. Say *a cup of tea* to yourself in both accents, and see how different they "feel" in the mouth.

Every language has its own consonant system, its own "inventory" of consonants. In English there are two versions of certain consonants: "voiced," in which there is sound from the vocal cords, and "voiceless" (or "unvoiced"), in which there is no vibration of the vocal cords. The pairs are, voiced and voiceless respectively: /b/ and /p/; /d/ and /t/; /j/ (/dg/) as in *edge* and /ch/ (/tsh/) as in *church*; /v/ and /f/; /g/ and /k/; /z/ and /s/; /zh/ as in *pleasure* and /sh/ as in *sure*; voiced /th/ as in *there* and voiceless /th/ as in *think*.

A letter is used in spelling to indicate what is actually a range of sounds. For example, the /t/ at the beginning of a word is actually a different sound from the /t/ in the middle of a word, different yet again from the sound at the end of a word: e.g., *tip, matter, pit*. In the more heavily "aspirated" version of /t/—that is, with breath added to the sound—sometimes heard in the middle of a word like *matter*, the tongue hardly touches the gum ridge and more air is forced through the vocal cavity; this is called a "tapped /t/." The "tapped /d/," heard as a substitute for voiced /th/ in some native and foreign accents in words like *other* and in some native accents in words like *whatever*, is also very important in accent work.

For all accents, native and foreign, always look at the consonants /l/, /r/, and /th / th/. These consonants are called "continuants," because their sounds can be continued as long as the speaker has breath. The /r/ sounds are especially important in any accent:

1. **Rhotic sounds:** Rhotic sounds are the voiced consonants spelled with the letter "r." (The word *rhotic* comes from the name of a Greek letter of the alphabet, *rho*.) The sound associated with this letter in another language is often carried into English in a foreign accent. Is "r" after a vowel—"post-vocalic"—pronounced, or is it as silent as the "b" in *lamb*? When post-vocalic letter "r" is pronounced, the accent is "rhotic"—as in a General American or Scottish accent. When post-vocalic "r" is not pronounced, the accent is "non-rhotic"—as in

a British RP accent. One of the first questions to ask when studying any accent is whether it is rhotic or non-rhotic.

2. **Native accents:** In English, /r/ is a "retroflex" consonant; that is, the tip of the tongue curls upward so that the bottom of the tongue is toward the palate when the sound is articulated. The hardness or softness of the sound depends on whether or not the back of the tongue is relaxed. For instance, in U.S. Midwestern accents it is slightly tensed, and in British RP it is relaxed. In accents native to English, if /r/ is not pronounced it still often influences the vowel that precedes it, because the tongue is beginning to curl upward as if to articulate an /r/, thus giving an impression of the letter /r/. Therefore, we speak of "r-influenced" vowels. In upper-class British English, post-vocalic /r/ is silent, with some exceptions. In General American, post-vocalic /r/ is pronounced, but it is silent in certain regional accents of the U.S., such as New York or some areas of the East Coast of the South. In some accents, among them British RP, Scottish, or certain Irish accents, a lightly trilled or tapped /r/ is sometimes heard.

3. **Foreign accents:** Is the /r/ in a foreign language trilled frontally, as in Italian or Spanish? Is /r/ pronounced from the back of the throat (a "uvular /r/"), as in French or German? Is /r/ pronounced in the middle of the mouth, with the tip of the tongue curving upward slightly so that the bottom of the tongue is toward the palate, as it is in General American or Mandarin?

4. **The trilled /r/:** To pronounce a trilled /r/ (with one or more taps or flaps) heard in many other languages, including Spanish, Italian, Swedish, Finnish, Basque, Portuguese, Polish, Russian, and Czech, begin by saying a tapped /d/: the tongue makes a minimal, quick pressure when the /d/ is articulated, as in the famous phrase *FuggeD-abouDit*. Then say the word *very* with a /d/ instead of an /r/. Draw the tip of the tongue back a very little bit and drop your tongue slightly until you have the impression of saying /r/. Do not curl the bottom of your tongue toward the roof of the mouth. The tip of the tongue

should be just at the opening of the palate in back of the gum ridge. Alternatively, you may begin a trilled /r/ by saying *hurrah* and shortening the vowel in the first syllable until it is entirely eliminated, leaving you with a very breathy sound: /hr/. Continue tapping the tip of the tongue lightly against the opening of the palate, hardly touching it at all. You can then eliminate the /h/.

5. **The uvular /r/:** To pronounce the uvular or guttural voiced /r/ heard in various versions in French, German, Yiddish, Dutch, Danish, Norwegian, and Hebrew, first lower the tip of the tongue so it touches the back of the lower front teeth, then raise the back of the tongue so the uvula vibrates against it, as in gargling, or as in articulating its voiceless version, the /kh/ sound heard in Scottish *loch* or German *Ach!* This consonant is, in fact, the voiceless one in the pair /kh/ and uvular /r/, which is a voiced consonant.

Some Questions to Ask Yourself

Select the accent to suit the character and make it your own by constant repetition and drilling. Whether you do a real or comically distorted accent, it must be organic and, therefore, internal to the character.

1. Is the accent rhotic or non-rhotic? In a foreign accent, does the native /r/ carry over into the accent in English?
2. How is /l/ pronounced—with the back of the tongue raised, as in Russian, or with the tip of the tongue well forward, as in French?
3. How are /th / *th*/ sounds pronounced—correctly, or are substitute sounds such as /d/ and /t/ used?
4. How do the vowels and diphthongs differ from your own accent?
5. What is the character's social and educational background? For instance, there are U.K. accents native to English associated with social classes.

6. If a character is from a foreign linguistic background, how did he or she learn English? A professor of physics who learned English at his European, African, or Asian university may speak with a more upper-class accent in English than a laborer who learned English on the streets of an English or American city. Did the character learn English at school, or on the streets of New York or London or Sydney or Johannesburg?

7. How well and how grammatically does the character speak the English language, as indicated in the script? This will often tell you how heavy the accent should be, whether it is native or foreign.

8. How thick or heavy or light is the accent? We sometimes hear such a slight accent that we cannot quite identify it. As an actor you may wish to create such an accent, or you may want to do an accent that is just a bit more identifiable to an audience. People can also be inconsistent within their own accent, and will sometimes pronounce /r/ or /th/ correctly, and sometimes not. As an actor, you should make sure that any accent you do is clearly understood, however thick the original may be in real life.

9. At what age did the person learn English? Below the age of twelve a heavy foreign accent is very rare, if indeed any exists at all. I know people who learned English as a second language, and grew up in New York City. They sound like New Yorkers speaking General American, and have not even a trace of the accent associated with their first language, which they also continue to speak. But even such brilliant people as Einstein and Freud, both of whom learned English comparatively late in life, spoke with very thick German and Viennese accents, respectively. Einstein even had to be subtitled in newsreels.

10. Where can I find actual examples of the accent, used by real people? You want to listen to and if possible record these examples. Embassies, consulates, movies, and restaurants with personnel who come from the country provide some excellent source material. Listening to a good dialect coach is all very well, but you want to

find actual examples and do the work yourself of analyzing what you are hearing.

An Exercise for Teaching Yourself Any Accent

You can use this exercise for studying the practice exercises and monologues at the end of each chapter.

When you know what the sounds of the accent are, and how they "shift" from the sounds you usually make, go through a script you are working on, a book you are reading, or any material you like, and select one sound. You might select /th / *th*/ substitutes, for instance, or a diphthong shift to a pure vowel, such as /oh/ to /aw/. Mark the sounds in some way, then go through the material again, speaking aloud and pronouncing only those sounds.

Do this for all the sound shifts, adding one each time. Do each new sound together with the ones you did previously. Eventually, you will have all the required sounds in place. Also, as you do this, be aware of exactly what the muscles of the mouth are doing, and you will concentrate on the correct positioning or placement of the lips, the tongue, and the opening of the mouth, wider or more closed as required.

You will thus become aware of how the whole accent that you have gradually built up feels in the mouth, and you can then make all of that into a habit.

When you have finished this part of the exercise, continue by writing out your own pronunciation using the list of phonetic symbols in this book, or the International Phonetic Alphabet (IPA), if you are familiar with it. Record yourself and listen carefully until you are satisfied that you have achieved the desired sound.

You will then be able to pick up any material and read it with the accent. Once you can do this, you have mastered the accent and it is now part of your actor's toolkit.

1
European Languages and Accents: General Advice and Useful Sounds

The Languages of Europe

Most European languages belong to the Indo-European family, divided into groups as follows, including:

1. **Albanian**, written in the Roman alphabet
2. **Baltic:** Two surviving languages, written in the Roman alphabet: Latvian, Lithuanian
3. **Celtic, also called Goidelic**, written in the Roman alphabet
   a. Current: Breton, Irish Gaelic, Scottish Gaelic, Welsh
   b. Extinct: Cornish, ancient Gaulish, Manx, ancient Pictish
4. **Germanic**, now written in the Roman alphabet, with the exceptions noted here
   a. Extinct: Proto-Germanic and several of its descendants, including Burgundian, Vandalic, and Gothic; modern descendants are listed below
   b. German, written in the Roman and, formerly, in the Old German (Gothic) alphabet; Yiddish, written in a modified Hebrew alphabet
   c. Dutch and its derivative, Afrikaans; Flemish, closely related to Dutch
   d. Old English (Anglo-Saxon) and its descendants: Modern English, Scots

e. Frisian: West and South Frisian, spoken on islands off the coast of Holland—the second most closely related of the Germanic languages to English after Scots

f. Old Norse, and its descendants: the Scandinavian languages Danish, Faroese, Icelandic, Norwegian, and Swedish

5. **Greek**, written in the Greek alphabet

6. **Italic**, written in the Roman alphabet

a. Latin

b. Latin's Romance language descendants: French, Spanish, Portuguese, Italian, Romanian; the less widely spoken Catalan, Gascon, Occitan, Provençal (the language of the medieval troubadours in France), Sardinian (with two dialects, and the closest of the Romance languages to Latin), Romansch (one of the four official languages of Switzerland), and Ladino, also known as Judezhmo or Judeo-Spanish (the medieval Jewish language still spoken around areas of the Mediterranean basin, consisting of Spanish with numerous Hebrew vocabulary elements)

7. **Slavic, also called Slavonic**

a. Old Bulgarian, which evolved into Old Church Slavonic, the liturgical language of several Eastern Orthodox churches; written in the Cyrillic alphabet devised by the Greek missionary monks Cyril and Methodius in the ninth century in what is now Bulgaria

b. Eastern Slavic, written in the Cyrillic alphabet: Russian, Belarusian, Ukrainian

c. South Slavic: Bulgarian (Cyrillic alphabet), Croatian (Roman alphabet), Slovene (also called Slovenian; Roman alphabet), Bosnian (written in both the Cyrillic and Roman alphabets)

d. Western Slavic languages, written in the Roman alphabet: Serbian, Polish, Czech, Slovak

Europe is also home to miscellaneous non-Indo-European languages, among them Basque, a true language isolate with no known relatives;

Hungarian; and Hungarian's possible distant Ural-Altaic relatives Estonian, Finnish, and the Sami languages of far northern Europe.

Naturally, in a book of this scope it is impossible to cover all these languages and their accents in English, so I have chosen those most useful for actors, which happen to be usually from the European languages that are most widely spoken around the world. Less widely spoken are Swedish (which does, however, have more speakers than the other Scandinavian languages) and Yiddish, which is, nevertheless, needed for a great body of American and British theatrical literature. For a more complete survey and details of the other European languages, see my book *Accents: A Manual for Actors* (revised and expanded edition; Limelight, 2002), in which Albanian, the Baltic languages, Basque, Finnish, Greek, Hungarian, and more Germanic, Romance, and Slavic language accents are detailed.

Important Features of the Language Groups Affecting Accents in English

Scottish and Irish accents descend, in part, from Scottish Gaelic and Irish Gaelic. These languages contributed specific sounds, and general rhythm and lilting intonation patterns that were carried over into English. Irish, Scottish, and Welsh accents are covered in my books *Accents: A Manual for Actors* and *Teach Yourself Accents—The British Isles* (Limelight, 2013).

Germanic language accents are characterized by even stressing of unstressed syllables; that is, most unstressed vowels have the same duration, while stressed vowels are lengthened, with sustained duration. This gives the accents their characteristic rhythm, and differentiates them from the Romance languages' rhythmic stressing, see chapter 2 on French accents.

The musical intonation patterns are the most salient feature of heavy Scandinavian accents in English: In Danish, this musicality is provided by lengthened vowels and glottal stopping, which is heard in Danish after many long vowels, whereas in English it is usually only heard as a replacement for the sound of /t/ in certain accents, such as Scottish, London Cockney, and the Bronx accent of New York City. The tones in Norwegian and Swedish must be heard pronounced by native speakers in order to be correctly imitated, and they sometimes carry over into a heavy accent in English. However, the expert language teaching in Scandinavia produces speakers with excellent English accents, and these tones are usually avoided.

One of the most important elements for the actor attempting to master Romance language accents is the phenomenon of "rhythmic phrasing": the habit of stressing one or more syllables in an entire phrase, rather than in an individual word, so that the stress in an individual word can shift depending on its position in the phrase, while the other syllables in the phrase are fairly even in duration. French is the most prominent example of a language in which rhythmic phrasing is the system of stressing, but all the Romance languages have this tendency to a greater or lesser degree, and transfer it into the rhythm of accents in English.

Slavic phonetics include two phenomena useful to know in doing Slavic language accents in English. First, there are the agglutinative consonants: combinations of consonants called "consonant clusters." While they vary from language to language, they condition the position of the vocal apparatus generally, as the tongue continues to seek a forward, upward position, in order to articulate the consonants. Secondly, certain consonants are "palatalized," especially in Russian; see chapter 5. This feature of the language can carry over into an accent in English.

There is also a typical Slavic /l/, heard in Russian, Serbo-Croatian, and other languages, articulated by pressing the tongue directly against the back of the upper front teeth while raising the middle of the tongue toward the palate. This is in addition to the dark liquid /l/, similar to the /l/ in French, also heard in Russian and in Polish. In Polish there is also an "l" written with a diagonal line through it: the sound of this consonant is close to the sound of the General American semi-vowel /w/.

Teach Yourself European Accents

Learn Some of the Language

When you do a European accent, learn some of the language. You will feel how the muscles of the mouth are used during speech, and you will be able to use the same placement of them when you do the accent in English. You will unconsciously absorb the correct positioning of the lips and tongue, and the feeling of where the vowels resonate and how hard or soft the consonants are. Use the foreign language sentences you learn in the practice exercises in each chapter to launch yourself into the accent: say them aloud, and without changing the position of the lips and jaw, immediately speak some of your lines in English.

It is also of paramount importance to learn the phonetic and orthographic systems of a parent language, including the use of diacritics (acute and grave accents, the cedilla, the tilde, etc.) that may alter the sound value of a letter, especially the ways in which they differ from English. Doing this will help you enormously in learning an accent: Each language attaches specific sounds to particular letters of the alphabet. It is often very difficult to eliminate from someone's accent certain ingrained phonetic traits that are also associated with the pronunciation of certain letters. For instance, in both British RP and General American, we voice final consonants in such words as *is* and *end*, but in German, the letters "s" and "d" are learned as voiceless sounds when used at the end of a word, so in a German accent in English they are often pronounced that way at the ends of English words—/IHS/, /ENT/—rather than with the voiced sounds native to English: /IHZ/, /END/. Sometimes, these consonants are not even heard as voiced by German speakers learning English; hence, the pronunciation that we hear as part of a German accent.

When Europeans learn the British RP accent, which is detailed in my book *Teach Yourself Accents—The British Isles*, their English pronunciation is non-rhotic: post-vocalic (after a vowel) /r/, spelled with the letter "r," is not pronounced—it is as silent as the "b" in *lamb*; and they use the British vowel system, pronouncing words spelled with the letter "a," such as *after*, *ask*, *bath*, *can't*, *dance*, and *master*, with the open-throated back vowel /ah/. But if your character learned Standard American English, use a General American accent, detailed in *Teach Yourself Accents—North America* (Limelight, 2013): Pronounce post-vocalic /r/, and use the American vowel system, pronouncing such words as *ask* and *can't* with the flat, closed vowel /a/.

The Sounds of /th / *th*/ and the Tapped /d/

Since the voiced /th/ in *that* and the voiceless /th/ in *think* do not exist in most European languages, there are similar consonants that are substituted, depending on the first language of the speaker. The usual substitutions are /z/ and /s/, /d/ and /t/, or (rarer) /v/ and /f/. See the individual chapters for details. See the introduction, too, for more information.

A version of the voiced /th/ does exist in Danish, and of the voiceless /th/ in Greek, as well as in the Castilian Spanish pronunciation of the letters "c" (before "e" and "i") and "z." It is, therefore, easier for speakers of these languages to learn the sounds correctly, but not everybody does so. Adopted by many speakers, a tapped /d/ is an easy substitute for voiced /th/, and is also heard in accents native to the English language.

To pronounce a tapped /d/, the tongue makes a minimal, quick pressure when the /d/ is articulated, rather than actually pressing hard, as it does for a fully articulated /d/. Try this with the phrase *good evening*, where the /d/ sound at the end of *good* is linked to the /ee/ in *evening* as a tapped /d/ sound: /goo DEEV nihng/.

The Intermediate Front Vowel /*ih*/

Learning the exact sound of the vowel /*ih*/ heard in so many European languages will provide you with one of your most useful tools. This version of the vowel /ih/ does not exist natively in English, and most European languages do not have the exact sound of English /ih/ in *bit*. But many languages have the sound of /ee/ in *meet*. So /ee/ is often substituted for /ih/.

The vowel sound heard in European languages is intermediate between /ih/ and /ee/; quite literally, the tongue is slightly lower in position than for /ih/ and slightly higher than for /ee/. Rather than being open, as they are for /ih/, the lips are slightly closed and protruded; nor are the corners pushed to the sides, as they are for /ee/. This intermediate front vowel /ih/ is the usual substitute for /ih/, and often for /ee/ as well.

The Sound of /u/

The sound of the English vowel /u/ in *but* and *love* does not exist in most other languages. The substitutions for it include /ah/ and /o/, or whatever seems closest to a vowel in the parent language that the person learning English can reproduce. See the individual chapters for these substitutions.

Substituting Monophthongs (Pure Vowels) for Diphthongs

Some European languages do not have the diphthongs /ay/ or /oh/, so unless these sounds are correctly learned, monophthongs (pure vowels) of sustained duration are substituted for them: *say* /SE/, *home* /HAWM/. For specific information, see the chapters on the different accents.

Rhotic Sounds

In most of the Romance languages, the trilled /r/ is used. In Standard French and in Standard High German, the /r/ is uvular, in the back of the throat. Learning these sounds gives you a useful tool for a great many accents in which one or the other /r/ is frequent, but not the American or British retroflex /r/. See the introduction for more information on these sounds, including how to pronounce them.

The Sounds of /l/

The sounds of /l/ are of primary importance in studying accents, as the /l/ of the parent language is often carried over into English. In all /l/ sounds, which are voiced consonants, the blade of the tongue (the little area just behind the tip) is raised and the tongue is slightly grooved; the tip and the blade of the tongue touch an area of the gum ridge near the upper front teeth and slightly block the opening behind the gum ridge into the hard palate. The back of the tongue is low, and air is allowed to pass above the back of and around the slightly retracted sides of the tongue; hence its characterization as a "lateral" consonant. Where the tip of the tongue is placed during the articulation of /l/ conditions how it sounds.

In the articulation of the American /l/ the contact of the tongue and the gum ridge is light, the tip of the tongue is placed just in front of the opening of the gum ridge where it starts to curve upward, and /l/ resonates in the same place as the vowel /e/.

For the formation of Russian /l/ sounds see chapter 5. Especially important is the palatalized Russian /l/ in which much of the tongue, including its middle, is raised to touch the roof of the mouth, creating a deep opening at the back. This /l/ is often heard not only in a Russian accent in English, but in some Scottish accents as well.

Different from either the American or Russian sounds, the French /l/ is pronounced with the front part of the tongue raised slightly as its tip lightly touches the upper gum ridge in front of where it curves into the upper palate, closer to the back of the upper front teeth than in forming an American /l/. The French /l/ is similar to the British and Irish /l/ sounds, in which the tongue is also more forward than it is in forming the American /l/.

A final word of advice: Keep things as simple as possible. Many Europeans speak excellent English, with only a slight accent that comes sometimes from the intonation patterns, or the rhythm, or from particular sounds. Sometimes an accent exists simply because a person maintains a general position of the mouth during speech that is not the natural position of a native English speaker—for instance, with the lips protruded slightly, and the muscles at the corners of the mouth slightly tensed, more so than in General American or British RP accents. Try to keep the accent light unless your character is supposed to have a heavy accent, and it will be that much more real.

The goal is to speak with your character's accent, without thinking about it, and in the most natural manner possible.

2
French Accents

French—an Indo-European language of the Romance family, descended from Latin—is spoken worldwide by about three hundred million people. It is the official language of the French Republic: Metropolitan France (Europe) and the Overseas Departments and Territories, among them French Guiana, Guadeloupe, Martinique, and French Polynesia. And it is one of the official languages of Belgium, Luxembourg, Switzerland, and Haiti. French is also one of the official languages of Canada, spoken most extensively in Québec Province and Acadie in New Brunswick. And French is a first language in parts of the United States, notably Maine and Louisiana, with its Cajun dialect. In thirty-one African countries, French is a first or second language, with varying vocabulary and accents, including those of Algeria, Tunisia, Morocco, Mali, Senegal, the Democratic Republic of the Congo, Côte d'Ivoire /KOT dee VWAHR/ (Ivory Coast), and Madagascar.

The most widely spoken dialect of French is non-regional Standard French, also sometimes called General French or Metropolitan French. It is taught in schools worldwide, and used in writing and the media. In Metropolitan France, it coexists with a dozen or more regional dialects and their accents, which condition the speakers' pronunciations in English. These accents include those of Paris, Lyon, Lille, Toulouse, Marseille, and other large cities, as well as provincial rural accents, among them those of Provence on the Mediterranean coast, and the Germanic-flavored accent of Alsace. In Lyon the accent is quite clipped, with short, clear vowels and hard consonants. Listen to the character of Monsieur Brun in Marcel Pagnol's *Fanny* (1932) for an authentic Lyon accent, and to the other characters for the salty, colorful, Italianate accent of Marseille, where the film takes place.

Belgium is also home to regional dialects and urban accents, and the pronunciation of French in Brussels is different, for instance, from that of the famously Flemish-influenced accent of Liège /LYEZH/. Belgian French is very clearly articulated, with stressed vowels lengthened slightly more and consonants softer than in France. The Swiss French accent of Geneva and Romandy, called in French the *Suisse romande* /süees ro MAHND/ (Romance Switzerland; the /ah/ is a nasalized vowel), is also very well articulated, with hard consonants and a tendency to draw out vowels slightly.

Haitians speak a French-based Creole, and most Haitians learn Standard French in school. For a Haitian French accent in English, substitute the intermediate front vowel /*ih*/ for the /ih/ in *bit*. And substitute /ah/ for the /u/ in *but* and *love*. For /th / *th*/ substitute /d/ and /t/. Do a retroflex /r/ or a uvular French /r/ if you want the accent to be heavier.

See my book *Teach Yourself Accents—North America* (Limelight, 2013) for more on Haitian French, and for the distinctive Canadian French accents. For a Québecois accent, substitute /d/ and /t/ for /th / *th*/. Do a retroflex /r/, or, for a heavier accent, a uvular or trilled /r/. Follow the advice on rhythmic phrasing discussed later in this chapter.

Characters with French accents in movies and on television include Hercule Poirot (Agatha Christie's Belgian detective), played by Peter Ustinov in *Death on the Nile* (1978) and *Appointment with Death* (1988), by Albert Finney in *Murder on the Orient Express* (1974), and by David Suchet on the television series *Agatha Christie's Poirot* (1989–2013). The French villagers in the British sitcom *'Allo! 'Allo!* (1982–1992), set in Nazi-occupied France, speak with fake French accents. And Peter Sellers concocted a hilarious accent for Inspector Clouseau in the Pink Panther film series, starting with *The Pink Panther* (1963).

For real French accents listen to Charles Boyer in *Gaslight* (1944), *Arch of Triumph* (1948), and many other movies, including Josh Logan's *Fanny*

(1961), also starring Leslie Caron and Maurice Chevalier. This non-musical film is based on the book for S. N. Behrman, Josh Logan, and Harold Rome's 1954 Broadway musical of the same name, adapted from Marcel Pagnol's Marseille trilogy of stage plays. You can also see Caron and Chevalier in the Vincente Minnelli–directed Lerner and Loewe musical *Gigi* (1958). This film also stars Louis Jourdan, who appeared in dozens of films, among them a television version of *Count Dracula* (1977), in which he plays the title role.

See Marcel Dalio in *Casablanca* (1942), *Sabrina* (1954), and *How to Steal a Million* (1966), and don't miss him in the French film *Entrée des artistes* (1938) /ahn tré dé zahr TEEST/ (literally, Entrance of-the Artists, or Stage Door; English title: *The Curtain Rises*), starring Louis Jouvet. Listen to Annabella in 13 *Rue Madeleine* (1947), Simone Signoret in *Ship of Fools* (1965), Gérard Depardieu in *Green Card* (1990), Lambert Wilson as the Marquis de Lafayette in *Jefferson in Paris* (1995), and Nathalie Baye in *Catch Me If You Can* (2002). And don't miss Jeanne Moreau, with her perfect English, superb in *I Love You, I Love You Not* (1996), and in her many French films, among them the François Truffaut classic *Jules and Jim* (1962). Emmanuelle Béart speaks excellent English in the film version of *Mission: Impossible* (1996), and be sure to see her in *Nelly et Monsieur Arnaud* /ne LEE e moo syoo ahr NO/ (1995), with the brilliant Michel Serrault, the original Albin in *La cage aux folles* /la kahzh o FOL/ (1978). (Note that the sound of /o/ represented by the French letter combination "au" does not have an exact equivalent in English: the phonetic symbol /o/ here represents a long, closed pure vowel with the lips rounded and well protruded. The letter "o" /o/ in the word *folles* represents a short closed pure vowel, uttered with corners of the lips tightened and slightly protruded.)

Translations of plays by Molière, Feydeau, and others require a correct pronunciation of names. Roles that require a French accent include the French Princess Katharine and her lady-in-waiting, who speak French as well as English with a French accent, in William Shakespeare's *Henry V* (1598–1599), and Dr. Caius in Shakespeare's *The Merry Wives of Windsor*

(1597). In Anna Cora Mowatt's American comedy of manners, *Fashion* (1845), Mrs. Tiffany has hired a French maid, Millinette, to teach her French manners. The *nouveau riche* hostess is eager to marry off her daughter to Count Jolimaitre, who turns out to be a fraud, complete with a phony French accent. Fake French accents are also used by Eisenstein and Frank, disguised as aristocratic guests at Prince Orlofsky's ball in Johann Strauss's classic Viennese operetta *Die Fledermaus* (1874).

Real French characters in plays include the Comtesse de la Brière in J. M. Barrie's *What Every Woman Knows* (1908) and Charmaine, the flirtatious tavern keeper's daughter in Maxwell Anderson and Laurence Stallings's World War I drama *What Price Glory?* (1924). She speaks English with the British soldiers while her father, Pierre, known as "Cognac Pete," speaks only French. Louise, the maid in Noël Coward's *Private Lives* (1930), speaks French. And in Terence Rattigan's comedy *French Without Tears* (1936), Professor Maingot and his daughter Jacqueline run a school in the south of France for English students who must speak only French while there; his part is almost entirely in French, although he occasionally speaks English with a heavy accent. Characters in plays set in the World War II years include Anise, the housekeeper for the Farrelly family, in Lillian Hellman's *Watch on the Rhine* (1941); Suzanne, Mme. Buffet, and others who help the Resistance in S. N. Behrman's *Jakobowski and the Colonel* (1944; filmed as *Me and the Colonel*, 1958); Emile de Becque, a planter on a South Pacific Island, who aids the war effort in Rodgers and Hammerstein's *South Pacific* (1949); and French civilians waiting at a detention center to be interrogated by German officers in Arthur Miller's *Incident at Vichy* (1964). More characters: General Jean-Jacques Dessalines and others, who do not necessarily have to speak with French accents, in Langston Hughes's *Emperor of Haiti* (1936); the French and Belgian Generals in Joan Littlewood's *Oh, What a Lovely War!* (1963); the French-Canadian political leader Louis Riel in John Coulter's *The Trial of Louis Riel* (1967); Mr. LaPoubelle in Israel Horovitz's *The Primary English Class* (1976); and Chauvelin, Marguerite, and other characters in Frank Wildhorn's Broadway musical *The Scarlet Pimpernel*

(1997), based on Baroness Orczy's novel. Orczy and her husband, Montague Barstow, wrote the 1903 play of the same name, on which she based her 1905 book. Lucille Cadeau, a film star invited to an English country village to open their annual garden fête, speaks only French in Alan Ayckbourn's very funny *House and Garden* (1999).

Teach Yourself French Accents

1. **Positioning, placement, and use of the muscles of the mouth during speech:** The Standard French language, and French accents in English, feel as if they resonate generally at the front of the mouth. The tongue is held up and forward, and its tip often almost touches the upper gum ridge. The lips are simultaneously protruded a bit and tensed slightly at the corners of the mouth. The mouth opening is fairly narrow much of the time.

2. **The sounds of /r/:** The /r/ in Standard French is uvular, formed in the throat. To pronounce the guttural or uvular /r/, first lower the tip of the tongue so it touches the back of the lower front teeth, then raise the back of the tongue to form a /g/; lower it, and allow the uvula to vibrate against it, as in gargling, or as in articulating its voiceless version, the /kh/ sound heard in Scottish *loch* or German *Ach!* The Parisian uvular /r/ is softer and more swallowed than the /r/ in Standard French, and this is the /r/ heard in a Parisian accent in English.

    a. **The trilled /r/:** Associated in France itself with non-standard rural speech, a frontal /r/ is also heard, with one trill. It is used as well in parts of Canada, such as Montreal. And a trilled /r/ is often used in French classical singing, especially French art song and opera. In popular song, comic opera and operetta, the uvular /r/ is more usual. See the introduction for tips on how to pronounce a trilled /r/.

b. **The retroflex /r/:** When your character pronounces the usual English and American retroflex /r/ with the tongue curled slightly upward toward the roof of the mouth, tense the back of the tongue slightly, and protrude the lips a bit, continuing this protrusion during the pronunciation of the vowel that follows or precedes /r/: this is the sound of the retroflex /r/ that is typically heard in a French accent.

3. **Vowels and diphthongs:** French has a larger vowel inventory than English, so there are vowels, semi-vowels, and diphthongs that do not exist in English, as well as many that do, with some important exceptions noted here.

a. **The intermediate front vowel /ih/:** This vowel is pronounced with the tongue slightly lower in position than for /ih/ and slightly higher than for /ee/. This vowel /ih/ is the usual substitute for /ih/, which does not exist in French, and often for /ee/ as well.

b. **Nasalized vowels:** In French spelling, a single "m" or an "n" often indicates that the preceding vowel is nasalized; the nasalized sound is the same for vowels preceded by either letter. This nasalization is sometimes transferred to English, especially in a heavy accent: *once* /WAHNS/, instead of /WUNTS/. Nasal vowels are pronounced by lowering the soft palate at the back of the mouth and allowing some air to flow through the nasal cavity just above it, without completing the articulation of the consonant; that is, without letting the lips press against each other when pronouncing /n/. In Southern French accents there is a tendency to denasalize nasal vowels, or, in Provence, to pronounce them as if they had /ng/ after them: *balcon* (balcony) Standard French: /bal KAWN/—the /AW/ is nasalized; Provence: /bal KAWNG/.

c. **The sound of /o/:** There is no exact equivalent to this sound in French. The vowel /o/ in *work* is usually pronounced with the lips strongly protruded, and vowels substituted for it include the

French vowel spelled "eu" as in *peu* /POO/ (little), and, less often, the vowels /e/ or /aw/.

d. **The sounds of /u/:** There is no /u/ vowel in French. Often substituted for it is a closed version of /o/, or /ah/: *but I love it* /bot I LOV *ih*t; baht I LAHV eet/.

e. **The mute "e" /uh/ (schwa):** What the French call an *e muet* /uh mü E/ (mute "e")—similar to the English schwa /uh/—is silent at the end of a word or syllable in Standard French, where it is spelled "e," serving simply as an indication that the consonant preceding it is pronounced. In singing, however, such syllables are usually set to music. And in Marseille and Provence, such syllables are frequently pronounced, giving the accent an Italian flavor. An example from Pagnol's *Fanny*: *Mais ça tombe très bien* (literally, But that falls very well, i.e., That's very opportune). In Standard French this is pronounced /mé sah tawmb trè BYEN/—with nasalized vowels in the syllables /tawmb/ and /BYEN/; in a Marseille accent: /me sah TAWM buh trè BYENG/, with no nasalization of the vowel in /TAWM/. If set to music, the Marseille pronunciation of *tombe* would be normal; not so, the /ng/ sound in *bien*.

f. **The sounds of the semi-vowels /w/ and /y/:** The French inventory includes the semi-vowels /w/: *oui* /WEE/ (yes); and /y/: *hier* /YER (alternatively, ee YER)/ (yesterday; the vowel /E/ is long). These semi-vowels are usually pronounced correctly in English: the initial letter "w" is pronounced /w/ in most words borrowed from English: *weekend* /*wih*k END/; but it is pronounced /v/ in many other French words: *wagon-lit* /vah gon LEE/ (sleeping car, on a train; the /o/ is nasalized).

4. **Other consonants:** The inventory of consonants is the same as in English, with the exception of /h/, /j/, and /th / th/, which do not exist in French. Initial consonants in French are soft, and final consonants, when pronounced, are hard. Importantly, this characteristic can carry over into an accent in English.

a. **The silent letter "h":** There is no /h/ sound in French, although the letter "h" is used in orthography, but when a word begins with "h," the "h" is not pronounced. In an accent in English /h/ is typically dropped: *him* /IHM/. But many people do learn to pronounce /h/ correctly. It is sometimes, although rarely, inserted where it is silent in English, or where it doesn't exist: *hour* /HOW uhr/ instead of /OW uhr/; [h]*all the time* /hawl duh TIM/ instead of *all the time* /AWL thuh TIM/.

b. **The shift of /j/ to /zh/:** There is no /j/ sound in French; the letter "j" is pronounced /zh/, and /zh/ is sometimes heard as a substitute for /j/ in a heavy accent: *judge* /ZHAHZH/, although /j/ is often learned correctly, so this substitution is rare.

c. **The sound of /l/:** The French /l/ is articulated with the front part of the tongue raised slightly as its tip lightly touches the upper gum ridge in front of where it curves into the upper palate, close to the back of the upper front teeth, but slightly away from them. It resonates where the front vowel /ih/ does. This /l/ is often heard in a French accent in English.

d. **The sounds of /th / *th*/:** There are no /th / *th*/ sounds in French, although the letter combination is used in orthography, and the sounds are often correctly learned. When they are not, substitute /z/ and /s/ or /d/ and /t/ for /th/ and /*th*/, respectively.

For a light accent, keep the general positioning of the mouth muscles consistent during speech, using the French position when speaking English. Pronounce the retroflex /r/ in the manner described above. To make the accent slightly heavier, use a French /l/ and a uvular /r/. And use the French stress patterns discussed here, but do not exaggerate them.

Intonation and Stress: The Music and Rhythm of the Accents

One of the most important features of a French accent in English is the stress pattern transferred from the French language. Both languages have primary and secondary stressing in phrases, sentences, and longer words. Importantly, a word in English retains its invariable stress no matter where it occurs; if the stress changes, the meaning changes, as with *INsult* (noun), and *inSULT* (verb). But stress in a French word is always variable, and depends on its position in a phrase.

The primary stress in a French phrase is always either on the last syllable or on the penultimate syllable when the last syllable contains a mute "e" (schwa). For example, in the phrase *une statue* /ün stah TÜ/ (a statue), the last syllable is stressed. In the phrase *une statue de marbre* /ün stah tü duh MAHR bruh/ (a statue of marble; a marble statue), the syllable spelled "tue" loses its stress, and the penultimate syllable, "mar," receives the stress, because the last syllable, "bre," contains a schwa.

This ubiquitous stress pattern in French is called "rhythmic phrasing"; a rhythmic phrase is also called a "stress group" or a "breath group." Such a phrase may consist of only one word: *Bonsoir!* /bawn SWAHR/ (Good evening!; the /aw/ is nasalized); but it usually consists of a group of words that form a logical grammatical entity, such as a noun with its adjectives.

When the French habit of rhythmic phrasing is transferred to English, it is often by giving primary stress to the last or penultimate syllable in a phrase, or by stressing all syllables in multisyllable words evenly, in an attempt to do them correctly. For example, *paper* might be pronounced /PE PUHR/, or *newspaper*, /NYOOHZ PE PUHR/. Where a native English speaker might say, "There was NOthing I could DO about it," a French speaker would tend to say, "There was NOthing I could do aBOUT it," or "There was nothing I could DO about IT."

There are several commonly heard intonation patterns that sometimes carry over into English. A question usually rises at the end. Uncertainty and negativity are often expressed by a falling tone at the end of an utterance. And a distinctive stressed pitch higher than the others may be used at the end of a declarative sentence to finalize the speaker's point.

Practice Exercises

Practice in French

1. *Bonjour. Comment allez-vous? Très bien, merci. Et vous?* [formal "you"]
/bawn ZHOOHR / ko mahn tah lé VOOH / trè BYEN mèr SEE / é VOOH/

Literal translation: Good-day. How go you? Very well, thanks. And you?
Translation: Hello. How are you? Very well, thanks. And you?

Notes: The vowels followed by "n" in *bonjour, comment*, and *bien* are nasalized. Notice the rhythmic phrasing, indicated by the stressed syllables. The /è/ in *très* is a very open sound.

2. From Marcel Proust's /mahr SEL PROOHST/ *Du côté de chez Swann* /dü ko TÉ duh shé SWAHN/ (*Swann's Way*; literally, Of-the Side of [In the Direction of] House-of Swann; 1913), "Première Partie, Combray" /pruh myèr pahr TEE kawm BRÉ/ ("First Part, Combray"; the vowel in the first syllable of *Combray* is nasalized)

Published in 1913, *Swann's Way* is the first volume of Marcel Proust's (1871–1922) masterpiece, *À la recherche du temps perdu* /ah lah ruh SHERSH dü tahn per DÜ/ (*In Search of Lost Time*; literally, To the Research of-the Time Lost; previously translated as *Remembrance of Things Past*). The novel, in which Swann is a principal character, is, among other things, a panoramic portrait of French society at the turn of the twentieth century. Combray is the village where the Narrator spends boyhood vacations, and the title refers to one of the walks the family takes in nice weather, in the direction of Swann's house. Here are the opening sentences.

Longtemps, je me suis couché de bonne heure. Parfois, à peine ma bougie éteinte, mes yeux se fermaient si vite que je n'avais

pas le temps de me dire: «Je m'endors.» Et, une demi-heure après,
la pensée qu'il était temps de chercher le sommeil m'éveillait; je
voulais poser le volume que je croyais avoir encore dans les mains
et souffler ma lumière . . .

/lawn TAHN zhuh muh süee kooh SHÉ duh bo NOOR / pahr FWAH ah
PEN mah booh zhee é TANT / mé ZYOO suh fer mé see VEET kuh zhuh
na vé pah luh tahn duh muh DEER / zhuh mahn DAWR / é ün duh mee
oo rah PRE / lah pahn SÉ kih lé te tahn duh sher shay luh so MEY mé ve
YÉ / zhuh vooh lé po zé luh vo LÜM kuh zhuh krwah yé ah vwahr ahn kawr
dahn lé MAN / é sooh flé mah lü MYER/

Literal translation: [For a] longtime, I myself have bedded [gone to bed]
of good hour [early]. Sometimes, to hard[ly] my candle extinguished, my
eyes themselves closed so quickly, that I had not the time to myself tell "I
myself fall-asleep." [I am falling asleep.] And a half hour after [later] the
thought that it was time to seek the sleep [to go to sleep] me awakened; I
wanted to-put-down the volume that I thought to-have still in the hands,
and to-blow-[out] my light . . .

Note: The vowels followed by "n" or "m" in *longtemps*, *éteinte*, *temps*,
m'endors, *pensée*, and *mains* are nasalized.

Practice in English
3. *It takes two hours to make this dish properly. Be sure when you serve it not
to put your arm in front of the customer's face. Don't argue with the customers.*

/eet teks tooh OW UHRZ tooh mek zees DEESH PRAW per LEE / bee
shooh wan yooh ser VEET naw tooh pot yooh HAHM een front ov zee kos
tih merz FES / dawn hahr GYOOH wee zee ko sto MER/

                              dish   ly.
                ho-   make this   prop-
          two   to   er-
  It takes   urs

                                                      face.
                                        cus-   mer's
                                arm   to-
                  serve it
    sure   you   not to put your   in front of the
  Be   when

          argue   cus-
  Don't   with the   to-
                              mers.

4. *Then you will take a piece of paper and write down your thoughts.*
Heavy accent: /zen (alternatively, den) yooh wi*h*l TEK uh p*ih*s ov PE PUHR (alternatively, PER) en rah dahn yooh SAWTS (alternatively, TAWTS, or *TH*AWTS)/

                                                thoughts.
  Then   per   write
        you   take a   pa-   down
              will   piece of   and   your

Three Scenes and One Monologue
1. From William Shakespeare's *Henry V* (1598–1599), Act 5, Scene 1
Henry V, the first king of England whose native language was English instead of French, has studied French a bit. And the French Princess Katharine has been studying English with her gentlewoman Alice. In the famous

wooing scene, Henry hopes to win Katharine's affections. He already has her hand in marriage, granted for political reasons.

KING HENRY. Fair Katharine, and most fair,
Will you vouchsafe to teach a soldier terms
Such as will enter at a lady's ear
And plead his love-suit to her gentle heart?
KATHARINE. Your Majesty shall mock me; I cannot speak your England.
KING HENRY. O fair Katharine, if you will love me soundly with your French heart, I will be glad to hear you confess it brokenly with your English tongue. Do you like me, Kate?
KATHARINE. Pardonnez-moi, I cannot tell what is "like me." [/pahr do né MWAH/ (Pardon me)]
KING HENRY. An angel is like you, Kate, and you are like an angel.
KATHARINE. Que dit-il? Que je suis semblable à les anges? [/koo dee T*IHL* / koo zhuh süee sahm BLAH blah lé ZAHNZH/ (What says he? That I am like the angels?)]
ALICE. Oui, vraiment, sauf votre grace, ainsi dit-il. [/WEE vré mahn sof vo truh GRAHS en see dee T*IHL*/ (Yes, truly, save your Grace, thus says he; the vowels /ah/ in /mahn/ and /e/ in /en/ are nasalized)]
KING HENRY. I said so, dear Katharine; and I must not blush to affirm it.
KATHARINE. O bon Dieu! les langues des hommes sont pleines de tromperies. [/o bawn DYOO / le lahngg dé ZOM sawn plen de trawm puh REE/ (Oh, good God! the tongues of men are full of deceits; the vowels in the syllables /bawn/, /lahngg/, /sawn/, and /trawm/ are nasalized)]
KING HENRY. What says she, fair one? That the tongues of men are full of deceits?

ALICE. Oui, dat de tongues of de mans is be full of deceits: dat is de Princess.

2. From William Shakespeare's *The Merry Wives of Windsor* (1597), Act 1, Scene 4

Young Dr. Caius /KA yoos/ (as usually anglicized) is a stereotypical choleric Frenchman, as the prejudiced English perceived the French to be. He resides in the town of Windsor, not far from London. Here, he is talking to the servant Simple and to Mistress Quickly, who helps keep house for him and is always at the Garter Inn. Sir Hugh is a Welsh parson, and Caius's rival for the hand of Anne Page, or so he thinks.

Shakespeare has clearly indicated the accent: /sh/ for /ch/ in *challenge* (in French orthography, "ch" is pronounced /sh/); /t/ for /th/ in *throat*; and /v/ for /w/ in *will*, which he sometimes pronounces /WIHL/ and sometimes /VIHL/. The substitution of /v/ for /w/ does reflect actual French pronunciation of the letter "w" at the beginning of many words or syllables. It is rare, however, since initial /w/ exists in French: *ouest* /WEST/ (west). The name Caius gives the Garter Inn is "Jartiere"—the French word for "garter" is *jarretière* /zhahr TYEHR/.

CAIUS. You jack'nape; give-a dis letter to Sir Hugh; by gar, it is a shallenge: I will cut his troat in de Park; and I will teach a scurvy jack-a-nape priest to meddle or make. You may be gone; it is not good you tarry here: by gar, I will cut all his two stones; by gar, he shall not have a stone to throw at his dog.

   (*Exit* SIMPLE.)

QUICKLY. Alas, he speaks but for his friend.

CAIUS. It is no matter-a ver dat:—do not you tell-a me dat I shall have Anne Page for myself? By gar, I vill kill de Jack priest; and I have appointed mine host of de Jartiere to measure our weapon. By gar, I vill myself have Anne Page.

3. From J. M. Barrie's *What Every Woman Knows* (1908), Act 2

What every woman knows in this pre-feminist play is that she is the power behind the throne, supporting the men in her life. A wealthy but uneducated Scottish family, the Wylies fear that their daughter Maggie will remain a spinster. The impoverished John Shand has been stealing into their house to read the books in their library, and when he is caught, he agrees to marry Maggie at the end of five years, if the Wylies will pay for his education. He does marry her, even though he does not love her, and she supports his rise to Parliament. But he falls in love with Lady Sybil Tenterden, who is encouraged to make a play for him by her French aunt, the Comtesse de la Brière /kawn tes duh lah bree ER/ (the vowel /aw/ in the first syllable is nasalized). Maggie is strong enough to let him go.

The Comtesse should have a light French accent, since her English is excellent, even though she does make a mistake in her second line.

COMTESSE. Don't you love a strong man, sleepy head?

SYBIL. (*Preening herself*) I never met one.

COMTESSE. Neither have I. But if you DID meet one, would he wakes you up?

SYBIL. I dare say he would find there were two of us.

COMTESSE. (*Considering her*) Yes, I think he would. Ever been in love, you cold thing?

SYBIL. (*Yawning*) I have never shot up in flame, Auntie.

COMTESSE. Think you could manage it?

SYBIL. If Mr. Right came along.

COMTESSE. As a girl of to-day it would be your duty to tame him.

SYBIL. As a girl of to-day I would try to do my duty.

COMTESSE. And if it turned out that HE tamed you instead?

SYBIL. He would have to do that if he were MY Mr. Right.

COMTESSE. And then?

SYBIL. Then, of course, I should adore him. Auntie, I think if I ever really love it will be like Mary Queen of Scots, who said of her Bothwell that she could follow him round the world in her nighty.

COMTESSE. My petite! [/puh TEET/ (little-one)]

SYBIL. I believe I mean it.

COMTESSE. Oh, it is quite my conception of your character. Do you know, I am rather sorry for this Mr. John Shand.

SYBIL. (*Opening her fine eyes*) Why? He is quite a boor, is he not?

COMTESSE. For that very reason. Because his great hour is already nearly sped. That wild bull manner that moves the multitude— they will laugh at it in your House of Commons.

SYBIL. (*Indifferent*) I suppose so.

COMTESSE. Yet if he had education—

SYBIL. Have we not been hearing how superbly he is educated?

COMTESSE. It is such as you or me that he needs to educate him now. You could do it almost too well.

4. From John Coulter's *The Trial of Louis Riel* (1967)

In 1869, to secure the rights and help preserve the culture and lands of the severely oppressed, discriminated-against Métis /mé TEES/—Francophone people of mixed French and Native descent—the politician Louis Riel /ree YEL/, a Métis himself, and a founder of the province of Manitoba, led the Red River Rebellion against the government of the Canadian Confederation, established only two years earlier. He fled to the United States, and even in exile was elected three times to the Canadian Parliament, in which he never sat. Returning to Canada, he led the Northwest Rebellion of 1885, again on behalf of the Métis. Riel was captured, put on trial for high treason, and hanged.

This semi-documentary account of his trial was performed most recently in May 2013 in Regina, Saskatchewan, by Rielco Productions, which has been presenting the play since 1967. You can see an excerpt on YouTube.

Here is part of Louis Riel's final speech in defense of his actions. He should have a light but distinctive Canadian French accent: Substitute /ih/ for /ih/, drop initial /h/, and substitute /d/ and /t/ for most /th / th/ sounds. To make the accent heavier, use a uvular /r/.

> RIEL. Today, although I am a man, I am as helpless before the Court of the Dominion of Canada, and in this world, as I was help-less on the knees of my mother on the day of my birth.
>
> The Northwest also is my mother. It is my mother country. And I am sure my mother country will not kill me . . . any more than my mother did, forty years ago when I came into this world. Because, even if I have my faults, she is my mother and will see that I am true, and be full of love for me.
>
> When I came into the Northwest in July, the 1st of July, 1884, I found the Indians suffering. I found the half-breeds eating the rotten pork of the Hudson's Bay Company. They were getting sick and weak every day. I also saw the whites. Although I am a half-breed, the greatest part of my heart and blood is white. So I wanted to help also the whites to the best of my ability. I worked for them here as I worked for them in Manitoba fifteen years ago. I can say that by the grace of God I am the founder of Manitoba. I was exiled for my pains. But today in Manitoba they have chosen institutions and I—I am here, hounded, outlawed, on trial for my life, forgotten in Manitoba as if I were dead.

3
German Accents

German, descended from Gothic, is an Indo-European language of the Germanic family, to which English also belongs, and is spoken as a first language by more than one hundred million people worldwide. Used in government, writing, and the media, it is the official language of Germany and Austria, and one of the official languages of Luxembourg and Switzerland.

The history of the standardization of German is complicated. Eventually, despite the numerous dialects spoken in the independent principalities and dukedoms, *Hochdeutsch* /HOKH DOYTSH/ ([Standard] High German) became the language of civil administration in the German-speaking lands, given an impetus by Martin Luther's sixteenth-century translation of the Bible, in which he used the administrative language of Saxony. Until around the middle of the eighteenth century, Hochdeutsch was mainly a written language, but for governmental and commercial reasons, it rapidly became a spoken standard dialect as well. For centuries, its Austrian German variant had been a commercial and administrative lingua franca throughout Eastern Europe, even before various countries were united politically under the Hapsburg monarchy of the Austro-Hungarian Empire, which ceased to exist at the end of World War I.

The standard non-regional accent of Hochdeutsch is based on educated, formal North German pronunciation patterns, and is taught worldwide. This pronunciation is sometimes known as *Bühnenaussprache* /BÜ nuhn OWS SHPRAH khe (alternatively, khuh)/ (stage-accent, or stage-pronunciation).

Regional pronunciations still exhibit great variety. Some of the principal dialects in Germany, all of which make a difference in the accents when speaking English (and contribute regional accents to Hochdeutsch), are those of Hanover and Prussia in the north, Bavaria in the southeast, Swabia in the southwest, and Saxony in the east. Berlin, Munich, and other large cities have their own urban accents.

In Austria, Vienna's colorful dialect—*Wienerisch* /VEE nuh r*ih*sh/ (Viennese)—has a lilting accent, while Austrian rural accents resemble those of Bavaria.

For acting purposes you will want to study the Prussian / North German and Austrian / South German accents. A Swiss German accent strongly resembles a Bavarian or Austrian accent, and *Schwyzertütsch* /SHVIH tsuh TÜTSH/ (Swiss German) is widely spoken, in a number of dialects.

For Prussian / North German accents listen to Sig Ruman, who was from Hamburg, as impresario Herman Gottlieb in *A Night at the Opera* (1935), "Concentration Camp" Ehrhardt in *To Be or Not to Be* (1942), and Sergeant Schulz in *Stalag 17* (1953; adapted from the Broadway play), with Berlin-born Erwin Kaiser, whom you can also see in *Watch on the Rhine* (1943). Felix Bressart, from East Prussia, is a wonderful character actor in such films as *To Be or Not to Be* and *The Shop Around the Corner* (1940), both of which were directed by Ernst Lubitsch. And see Conrad Veidt, born in Potsdam, in Michael Curtiz's *Casablanca* (1942) and many other films; Marlene Dietrich, from Berlin, in George Marshall's *Destry Rides Again* (1939) and more than fifty films; Mannheim-born Albert Basserman in Alfred Hitchcock's *Foreign Correspondent* (1940) and Michael Powell's *The Red Shoes* (1948); Armin Mueller-Stahl, from East Prussia, in Barry Levinson's *Avalon* (1990) and Scott Hicks's *Shine* (1996); Lilli Palmer, with a very light accent, from Posen in East Prussia, in George Seaton's *The Counterfeit Traitor* (1962); Berlin-born Horst Buchholz in John Sturges's *The Magnificent Seven* (1960); and Gert Frobe, born in Zwickau, Saxony, in Guy Hamilton's *Goldfinger* (1964) and René Clément's *Is Paris Burning?* (1966).

For Austrian / South German accents, listen to the following actors, all from Vienna: Walter Slezak in Hitchcock's *Lifeboat* (1944); Anton Walbrook in Michael Powell's *49th Parallel* (1941) and as the ballet impresario in *The Red Shoes*; Oskar Homolka and Helmut Dantine in King Vidor's *War and Peace* (1956); Maria Schell in *The Heart of the Matter* (1953); her brother Maximilian Schell in *Cross of Iron* (1977); Otto Preminger as the Camp Commandant in *Stalag 17* and the German Consul in *Margin for Error* (1943; Preminger also directed the film, adapted from the Broadway play), co-starring Carl Esmond; Lotte Lenya in *From Russia with Love* (1963); and Oskar Werner in *Ship of Fools* (1965). Born in Trieste but raised in Vienna, Paul Henreid has a pleasant, light accent. See him in *Casablanca*, the 1940 film *Night Train to Munich* (billed as Paul von Hernried, his original aristocratic name), and *The Conspirators* (1944) with Hedy Lamarr, who has the lightest of Viennese accents, as does Christoph Waltz in Quentin Tarantino's *Inglourious Basterds* (2009) and *Django Unchained* (2012). Also from Vienna is Klaus Maria Brandauer, who plays a Swedish baron in *Out of Africa* (1985). Don't miss him as a stage actor in Nazi Germany in the Hungarian-made German-language film *Mephisto* (1981). For a more rural accent, listen to Arnold Schwarzenegger, from the small town of Tahl in the Austrian province of Styria, in his many action-adventure films. And listen to the Munich / Bavarian accent of Curd Jürgens (billed as Curt Jurgens) in *Battle of Britain* (1969) and *The Spy Who Loved Me* (1977).

Among roles requiring German accents are Mrs. Fiorentino in Elmer Rice's *Street Scene* (1929); Rudolph Kammerling, the film director, in Kaufman and Hart's *Once in a Lifetime* (1930); the flea circus professor Jonas in Ben Hecht and Gene Fowler's rarely revived Depression-era play *The Great Magoo* (1932); and Feydak, the Viennese composer in S. N. Behrman's *Biography* (1932).

Plays set during the World War II years include many German characters, among them the Consul, the Baron, and others in Claire Boothe's *Margin for Error: A Satirical Melodrama* (1939); Dr. Hermann Walther, the Nazi in Elmer Rice's *Flight to the West* (1940); Kurt Muller and the three

Muller children in Lillian Hellman's *Watch on the Rhine* (1941); the teenager Emil Bruckner, and the Frame family's maid, Frieda, in John Gow and Arnaud d'Usseau's *Tomorrow the World* (1943); and the POW camp personnel in Donald Bevan and Edmund Trzcinski's *Stalag 17* (1951), based on the authors' experiences as prisoners of war. In Tennessee Williams's *The Night of the Iguana* (1961), set in 1940s Mexico, we meet the nationalistic tourists Herr and Frau Fahrenkopf, and in Israel Horovitz's *The Primary English Class* (1976), Mr. Mulleimer is an immigrant to the U.S. German accents are necessary in Kander and Ebb's Broadway show *Cabaret*, set just prior to the war, and first produced in 1966. They are required as well in John Bishop's hilarious spy spoof *The Musical Comedy Murders of 1940* (1987), and in Ronald Harwood's *Taking Sides* (1995), about the interrogation by an American army officer of the German conductor Wilhelm Furtwängler, just after World War II.

Teach Yourself German Accents

1. **Positioning, placement, and use of the muscles of the mouth during speech:** The German language, and North and South German accents in English, feel as if they resonate generally near the front of the mouth. The tongue is held up, and slightly tensed, with its tip forward. The lips are often protruded slightly, with the corners of the mouth tensed. The mouth opening is narrow much of the time.

2. **The sounds of /r/:** There are two rhotic sounds used in the different German accents:

   a. **The uvular /r/:** In North German accents, the uvular /r/ is generally lightly guttural (in the throat), and sometimes heavily guttural. See the previous chapter, on French accents, for its proper pronunciation.

b. **The trilled /r/:** In Austrian / South German accents, such as those of Vienna and Bavaria, /r/ is given a frontal trill (usually one flap). See the introduction for tips on how to pronounce a trilled /r/.

3. **Vowels and diphthongs:** The German vowel and diphthong inventory is much the same as in English, with exceptions noted below, and also includes sounds that do not exist in English. In Vienna, many vowels are diphthongized and lengthened. This characteristic is transferred into an Austrian accent in English.

   a. **The shift from /a/ to /e/:** The sound of the vowel /a/ in *that* does not exist in German, so /e/ is usually substituted for /a/ in a heavy German accent: *cab* /KEP/, *cap* /KEP/, *had* /HET/, *hat* /HET/, *handle* /HEN duhl/, *magnificent* /ME gnih fih SUHNT/.

   b. **The intermediate front vowel /ih/:** The vowel /ih/ does not exist in German, and the usual substitute for it is /ih/, with the tongue and mouth opening in a position between that for /ee/ and /ih/.

   c. **The shift from /u/ to /ah/:** There is no /u/ sound in German, and the usual substitution in an accent in English is /ah/: *but* /BAHT/, *love* /LAHF/.

   d. **Other vowel substitutions:** Substitute the lengthened pure vowel /aw/ for the diphthong /oh/, and the lengthened pure vowel /e/ for the diphthong /ay/.

   e. **Diphthongization of vowels in a South German / Austrian accent:** In South German / Austrian accents, diphthongize pure vowels, especially before /r/. In Viennese German, for example, /ah/ shifts to /aw/, and before /r/ to a diphthongized /AWuh/. This carries over into English: Substitute /aw/ for /ah/ in words like *father* (occasionally), and diphthongize /aw/ before /r/: *of course* /uf KAWuhS (alternatively, KOOHuhs)/. The vowel /ooh/ is also diphthongized: *sure* /SHOOHuh (alternatively, SHOOHah)/.

4. **Other consonants:** The German inventory of consonants is the same as in English, with the exception of /j/, /zh/, and /th / *th*/, which do not exist in German; other exceptions are noted below. It

is important to remember that in German orthography the letters of the alphabet are used differently than in English orthography. Initial semi-vowels and consonants have different sounds associated with the letters of the alphabet than they do in English. In heavy accents, use the German sounds for the letters.

a. **Devoiced final consonants:** The sound values attached to certain letters at the ends of English words stand for voiced consonants: they include "b," "d," "g," "s" (heard as /z/), and "v." (The letter "z" stands for /ts/ in German, but Germans learn the correct sound, /z/, except at the end of a word, where it is devoiced to /s/.) These same letters all denote voiceless consonants at the end of words in German, and the letters stand for the sounds /p/, /t/, /k/, /s/, and /f/, respectively. This characteristic is transferred to an accent in English, and is usually the last thing to disappear, so use it even in a very light accent. Examples: *ballad* /BE let/, *beans* /BIHNTS (alternatively, BEENTS)/, *bend* /BENT/, *bide* /BIT/, *bins* /BIHNTS/, *blood* /BLAHT/, *cab* /KEP/, *end* /ENT/, *England* /IHNG (alternatively, ENG) lahnt/, *give* /GIHF/, *had* /HET/, *have* /HEF/, *haze* /HAYS/, *is* /IHS/, *pad* /PET/, *that* /DET, or ZET/, *was* /VAHS/.

   As if in compensation, in an exaggerated comic German accent, some final voiceless consonants shift to voiced: *it's true* /IHDZ TROOH/, *that's right* /DEDZ RID/. The guttural or trilled /r/ should be used as well.

b. **Some initial consonants:** Certain initial voiced consonants are devoiced, especially before /r/ in a heavy German accent, so that, for instance, /d/ shifts to /t/: *dry* /TRI/; /g/ shifts to /k/: *grand* /KRENT/; and /p/ shifts to /b/: *prove* /BROOHF/.

c. **The sound of /h/:** There is an initial /h/ sound in German, spelled "h," so there is no problem doing this accurately in an accent in English.

d. **The shift of /j/ to /ch/:** Because /j/ does not exist in German, /ch/ is often substituted for it, especially in a heavy accent: *edge* /ECH/, *German* /CHO mahn/, *just* /CHAHST (alternatively, CHOST)/.

e. **The sound of /l/:** In Standard High German, this consonant is similar to the French /l/, and is the /l/ often heard in German accents in English; see the previous chapter for tips on how to pronounce this /l/. It resonates where the front vowel /ih/ does.

f. **The shift from /s/ to /z/:** In German orthography, a soft version of the sound /z/ is attached to the letter "s" at the beginning of a word, so use /z/ in a very heavy accent in English: *so* /ZOH/, *sun* /ZUN/. And use a light /z/ or the correct /s/ for a much lighter accent.

g. **The sound of /sh/:** The consonant /sh/, spelled in German orthography "sch" or "s" before "p" or "t," is pronounced with the lips protruded, unlike its English counterpart. Use this protrusion when doing an accent in English on any word with /sh/, such as *shy*, *sugar*, or *sure*.

h. **The sounds of /th / *th*/:** The consonants /th/ and /*th*/ do not exist in the German language, although the letter combination "th" is used in spelling. In North German accents, substitute /z/ for /th/ and /s/ for /*th*/: *this thing* /ZIHS SIHNG/. In South German accents, substitute /d/ and /t/: *this thing* /DIHS TIHNG/. Between vowels /th/ is sometimes heard as an aspirated tapped /d/: *father* /FAH duh/.

i. **The occasional shift from /v/ to /f/:** In German orthography, the letter "v" at the beginning of a word is close in sound to English /f/, and this often carries over into a heavy accent in English: *very* /FE ree/, with either a uvular or trilled /r/. Occasionally, you might hear an initial /w/ substituted for /v/: *very* /WE ree/.

j. **The shift from initial /w/ to /v/ and the occasional shift from /v/ to /w/:** The sound of the semi-vowel /w/ does not exist in German. In German orthography, the letter "w" stands for the sound /v/, which is formed with less pressure of the upper teeth against the inside lower lip than in English. You should use this softer German /v/ at the beginning of a word in

an accent in English: *one* /VAHN/, *when* /VEN/, *won* /VAHN/.
When the combination "qu" is used in English spelling it is pronounced /kw/, a sound that also does not exist in German, even
though the letter combination "qu" is used in German spelling. In
a German accent in English, the sounds /kv/ or /kf/, with which
the letter combination is associated in German, are substituted
for /kw/: *queen* /KVEEN (alternatively, KFEEN)/, *quite* /KVIT
(alternatively, KFIT)/, *Queen Elizabeth the Second* /KFEEN e LIH
zah BET zuh ZEK (alternatively, SEK) uhnt/, in a heavy North
German accent.

   Occasionally, initial /v/ shifts to /w/ in a very heavy accent: *visit* /WIH ziht/, *invite* /ihn WIT/. But this is by no means always done.

k. **The shift from /zh/ to /sh/**: Because /zh/ does not exist in German, /sh/ is often substituted for it in a heavy accent: *pleasure*
/PLE shuh/.

l. **Non-English sounds:** Although these sounds do not occur in
English, it is useful to know them when you have to say certain
words in German. There is a German /kh/, spelled "ch" in German.
There are soft and hard versions: the hard sound, as in German
Ach!, is like Scottish *loch* /LOKH/. The soft sound is close to the
English initial /h/ or to the Spanish letters "j" and "x"—both pronounced /kh/—in such German words as *Ich* /IHKH/ (the first-
person pronoun "I") and *fertig* /FE[R] tihkh/ (finished), dialecti-
cally pronounced sometimes, for example in Berlin, as a /k/. To
pronounce it correctly in German, say the English word *hue*, then
add the sound /ih/ before *hue*, then drop the "ue."

For a light accent, keep the general positioning of the mouth muscles consistent during speech, using the German position when speaking English,
and using German intonation patterns; devoice final consonants, and
pronounce the initials /w/ and /s/ correctly. Use a retroflex /r/ with the tip
of the tongue farther back than in most natively pronounced /r/ sounds.

Use either the British RP or General American vowel system, depending on the accent of English your character learned.

Intonation and Stress: The Music and Rhythm of the Accents

Stress in German has complicated rules. For a German accent in English, stress words correctly.

In German, as in English, there are primary and secondary stresses in longer words. Unstressed syllables in German, unlike those in English, are all usually even in duration, except for those containing a schwa, which makes the syllable short. This pattern is carried over into the rhythmic pattern of an accent in English.

In Standard High German, as in English, stressed syllables are on a differentiated pitch, and their vowels are lengthened. In German intonation, after a stressed syllable spoken on an upper pitch, the following syllables usually drop in pitch. A typical intonation pattern consists of a rising tone on a stressed word in a declarative sentence, while the tones around it are spoken on the same low level. This pattern can be transferred into a German accent in English, as in the following example: "That is quite RIGHT, I think." All the unstressed syllables, lower in pitch than the stressed syllable, are of fairly even duration, while the stressed syllable, higher in pitch, is longer.

In Vienna, Wienerisch has a sing-song lilt that even tram conductors use when announcing stops on the *Ringstrasse* /RIHNG SHTRAH se (alternatively, suh)/ (Ring-street): *Nächste Anhalt, Schottentor!* (Next stop, Scottish-Gate); Viennese pronunciation: /NEKH stuh AWN HAWLT SHAWT ten TOOHuh/; Hochdeutsch pronunciation: /NEKH stuh AHN HAHLT SHOT ten TAW/; the /kh/ in both pronunciations is soft.

```
        ste                 ten-
   Näch-         halt,
           An-                    r!
                   Schot-    to-/
```

Be sure to use the intermediate front /ih/ vowel on the first syllable, /RIHNG/. And notice the typical Viennese vowels and diphthongs in the pronunciation: the shift from /ah/ to /aw/, and the diphthongization of the "o" in "-tor." You can hear this Viennese lilt and the wonderful Wienerisch accent in the dialogue of Johann Strauss's *Die Fledermaus*, on the 1960 London recording (421 046-2) conducted by Herbert von Karajan.

Practice Exercises
Practice in German
1. *Guten Tag. Wie geht es Ihnen? Sehr gut, danke. Und Ihnen?* [formal "you"]
North German / Prussian: /GOO tuhn TAHK (alternatively, TAKH) / vee GET es EE nen / ZE[R] GOOHT DAHN ke (alternatively, kuh) / oont EE nen/
Austrian: /GOO duhn TAWK / vee GE duhs EE nen / ZEEuh GOOHT DAWN ke (alternatively, kuh) / oont EE nen/

Literal translation: Good day. How goes it with-you? Very good, thanks. And you?
Translation: Hello. How are you? Very well, thanks. And you?

Notes: The word *Ihnen* in the sentence *Wie geht es Ihnen?* is the third person plural pronoun "they," in the dative case—"with" or "to them"—meaning "you," however, in the most formal contemporary address. The final /kh/ in the word *Tag* is a soft version of the consonant heard in *Ach!*, but not the same soft version heard in *Ich*. The vowel in the syllable /GET/ is of sustained duration, like all the vowels in the Austrian pronunciation as well. Notice the tapped /d/ in the syllable /duhs/ in the Austrian pronunciation. The /t/ at the end of /GOOHT/ is either distinct, or assimilated into the /d/ of *danke*. The /aw/ in /DAWN/ is nasalized; see the information in chapter 2 on French accents.

2. From Johann Wolfgang von Goethe's /YO hahn VOLF gahng fon GO tuh/ *Die Leiden des jungen Werther* /dee LI duhn des YOONG en VE[R] tuh[r]/ (*The Sorrows of Young Werther*; 1774), Erstes Buch /ER stuhs BOOKH/ (First Book)

This is the opening of the quintessential Romantic novel by Goethe (1749–1832), one of the greatest German writers, estheticians, and philosophers, and an enlightened humanist known also for *Faust*, a two-part dramatic poem. *The Sorrows of Young Werther* (1774), a largely epistolary, semi-autobiographical narrative, tells the story of the unhappy love of the passionate artist Werther for Charlotte, who is married, and ends with Werther committing suicide. He has fled the scene in despair, and is writing to his closest friend, Wilhelm /*VIHL* HELM/ (William). Jules Massenet's opera *Werther* (1892) captures the story with compelling drama and heartbreaking music.

The schwa /uh/ in the final syllable of "Werther" is r-influenced, so that a very slight /r/ is heard. Notice the German letter "ß," which is "ss," in the words "daß" /DAHS/ (that), also spelled "dass," and "weiß" /VIS/ (know), also spelled "weiss." German nouns are capitalized.

> Am 4. Mai 1771 [Am vierten Mai siebzehnhunderteinundsiebzig] Wie froh bin ich, daß ich weg bin! Bester Freund, was ist das Herz des Menschen! Dich zu verlassen, den ich so liebe, von dem ich unzertrennlich war, und froh zu sein! Ich weiß, du verzeihst mir's.

/ahm FEE[R] tuhn MI *ZIHP* tsen HOON duht INTS oont *ZIHP* tsihkh / vee FROH bi*hn IHKH* dahs *ihkh* VEK B*II*IN / BE stuh FROYN'I' / vahs *ihst* dahs HE[R]TS des MEN shuhn / D*IHKH* tsooh fe[r] LAH suhn den *ihkh* ZOH LEE buh / fon DEM *ihkh* OON tse[r] TREN l*ihkh* VAH[R] / oont FROH tsooh ZIN / *ihkh* VIS dooh fe[r] TSIST MEEuhs/

Literal translation: On-the 4 May, 1771. How happy am I, that I away am! Best friend, what is the heart of-the men [mankind]! You to abandon, whom I so love, from whom I inseparable was, and happy to be! I know you forgive me it.

Note: The /e/ in the pronunciation syllables /tsen/, /den/, and /DEM/ is lengthened and therefore of sustained duration.

Practice in English
3. *It would have been quite something if what I had said had really happened.*
Very heavy accent: /*ih*t VOOT hef been KVIT ZUM *sih*nk *ih*f vaht I het ZET het REEuh lee HEP uhmt/
Medium heavy accent: /*ih*t VOOT haf been KFIT SUM *sih*nk ihf vaht I het SET het REE lee HEP ent/
Lighter accent: /*ih*t WOOT hef been KWIT SUM *sih*nk ihf waht I hat set hat REE lee HAP ent/
Lightest accent: /iht WOOT haf bihn KWIT SUM *thi*hng ihf waht I hat SET hat REE lee HAP uhnt/

Notes: Notice the devoiced final consonants in all the pronunciations. In words like *really*, draw out the diphthongs for Austrian accents; shorten them for North German accents. You will notice also in the pronunciation guide for the very heavy accent that the last syllable is /uhmt/ instead of the /uhnt/ you might expect. This is because in German a "-ben" word ending, as in the infinitive *haben* /HAH ben/ (to have), is often elided in everyday speech to /bm/, with the /b/ almost silent: /HAH bm/; and /p/ is the devoiced consonant that pairs with /b/. This pronunciation may sometimes be carried over into a German accent in English for words ending in "-ben" or "-pen."

4. *It is with great gratitude that I accept this award.*

Prussian / North German heavy accent: /*iht ihs* vihs KRAYT KRE t*ih*
TYOOHT zet (alternatively, set) I ek ZEPT z*ihs* e VAWT/
Austrian / Bavarian heavy accent: /*iht ihs* vi*ht* GRAYT GRE t*ih* TYOOHT
det I ek SEPT d*ihs* ah VAWuhT/

```
                  titude
        gra-                 cept        ward.
It is with great         that I ac-   this a-
```

Two Scenes and Two Monologues

1. From George S. Kaufman and Moss Hart's *Once in a Lifetime* (1930), Act 2

In this hilarious satirical farce guying the Hollywood movie industry, the imported German film director Rudolph Kammerling—choleric, frustrated, imperious, and opinionated—tries to contact his elusive producer Herman Glogauer, a movie mogul, through Glogauer's secretary, the ever-stoic, put-upon Miss Leighton.

MISS LEIGHTON. He's on Number Eight, Mr. Kammerling.
KAMMERLING. I just come from Number Eight—he is not there.
MISS LEIGHTON. Then he must be in conference with the exploitation people, Mr. Kammerling.
KAMMERLING. Maybe he is just through. Try his office.
MISS LEIGHTON. I've just come by there. He isn't in his office.
KAMMERLING. Gott in Himmel, he must be *some* place. Try Number Eight again. [/GOT *ihn* HIH muhl/ (God in heaven)]
MISS LEIGHTON. Yes, sir.
KAMMERLING. (*Pacing nervously up and down*) For two cents I would go back to Germany and Ufa! [/OOH fah/]
MISS LEIGHTON. (*At 'phone*) Number Eight! Mr. Kammerling calling Mr. Glogauer. Imperative!

KAMMERLING. America! Reinhardt begged me not to come. On his knees in the Schauspielhaus he begged me! [/SHOW shpeel HOWS/ (theater)]

MISS LEIGHTON. Hello? Mr. Glogauer not there? Just a moment . . . He isn't there, Mr. Kammerling. Any message?

KAMMERLING. (*Beside himself—shouting*) Yes! Tell them I take the next boat back to Germany! Wait! Who is it on the phone?

MISS LEIGHTON. Mr. Weisskopf.

KAMMERLING. Give it to me! (*Takes the phone;* MISS LEIGHTON *leaves.*) Hello! This is Kammerling . . . How much publicity is there sent out on Dorothy Dodd? . . . What? . . . We are lost! . . . Why? I tell you why! Because I have just seen her and she is impossible! I will not ruin my American career! . . . (*Hangs up*) What a country! Oh, to be in Russia with Eisenstein! (*He storms out.*)

Notes: Number Eight is a soundstage. "Ufa," also spelled "UFA" (Universum Film AG /OOH nee FER zoom F*I*HLM AH GE/), is a German film company; started in 1917, it was the principal German film studio until 1945, and is still making films and television programs. The abbreviation "AG" stands for *Aktiengesellschaft* /AHK tsee uhn guh ZEL SHAHFT/ (literally, shares company; public shareholders' corporation). Max Reinhardt /RIN HAHRT/ (1873–1943) was a great, influential, innovative Austrian stage director, forced to flee Nazi Germany because of his Jewish ancestry. He went to Hollywood, where he made one film, Shakespeare's *A Midsummer Night's Dream* (1935), co-directed by fellow Reinhardt protégé William Dieterle. Sergei Eisenstein /syer (alternatively, ser) GAY I zuhn SHTIN (alternatively, STIN)/ (1898–1948) was a great Soviet Russian film director, known (when *Once in a Lifetime* was produced) for his silent masterpiece *Battleship Potemkin* (1925).

2. From Lillian Hellman's *Watch on the Rhine* (1941), Act 2

After twenty years abroad, Sara Muller, daughter of the wealthy diplomatic Farrelly family, returns to her childhood home near Washington, DC, with her anti-Nazi German husband, Kurt Muller, and their three children. The reunion with her mother and brother is a joyful one. But for compelling reasons, Kurt, who worked with the German underground, decides that his real place is with the resistance movement. He will return home at the risk of his life. In this excerpt, Kurt, who had fought in the Spanish Civil War of 1936, talks about the song sung by the anti-Fascist Germans fighting in Spain.

In the 1943 film adaptation (directed by Herman Shumlin, and starring Bette Davis as Sara), Paul Lukas (who was actually from Budapest, Hungary) reprised his Broadway role as Kurt. Note that all the /kh/ sounds in the song are the soft version detailed earlier in this chapter.

> KURT. This is the way you heard it in Berlin in 1918. (*Begins to sing in German*)
> "Wir zieh'n Heim, wir zieh'n Heim.
> Mancher kommt nicht mit,
> Mancher ging verschütt,
> Aber Freunde sind wir stets."
> [/veeuh TSEEN HIM / veeuh TSEEN HIM/ (We come home, we come home)
> /MAHN khuh KOMT ni*h*kht M*I*HT/ (Many come not with [us])
> /MAHN khuh G*I*HNG fuh SHÜT/ (Many went lost [disappeared; snuffed it])
> /AH buh FROYN de Z*I*HNT veeuh SHTETS/ (But friends are we still)]
> (*In English*)
> "We come home, we come home.
> Some of us are gone, and some of us are lost, but we are friends:
> Our blood is on the earth together.
> Some day. Some day we shall meet again.
> Farewell."
> (*Stops singing*) At a quarter to six on November 7th, 1936, eighteen years later, five hundred Germans walked through the Madrid

streets on their way to defend the Manzanares [/mahn sah NAH res/] River. We felt good that morning. You know how it is to be good, when it is needed to be good? So we had need of new words to say that. I translate with awkwardness, you understand. (*Begins to sing again in English*)

"And so we have met again.

The blood on the earth did not have time to dry.

We need to stand and fight again.

This time we fight for people."

3. From James Gow and Arnaud d'Usseau's *Tomorrow the World* (1942), Act I

Emil Bruckner, a German teenager, has been sent to stay with his uncle, Professor Michael Frame, and his family in a Midwestern university town. Holding a telegram that has just been delivered, the Frames' German maid, Frieda, comes into the living room and discovers that Emil has come downstairs dressed in a Nazi uniform. She is horrified. In the 1944 film adaptation by Ring Lardner, Jr., and Leopold Atlas, Professor Frame is played by Fredric March, with Edit Angold (from Berlin) and Skippy Homeier reprising their Broadway roles as Frieda and Emil.

FRIEDA. You are insane!

(*She turns to go.*)

EMIL. *Halt!* [/HAHLT/]

(FRIEDA *stops.*)

Ich will mit Dir sprechen. Ich habe sofort gemerkt dass Du für das Vaterland arbeitest. [/*ihk*h VIHL m*ih*t DEE uh SHPRE khuhn / *ihk*h HAH buh zo faw[r]t ge ME[R]KT dahs dooh fü[r] dahs FAH tuh LAHNT ah BI test/ (I want with you to-speak. I have immediately noticed that you for the Fatherland work; note that the first "o" /o/ in the word *sofort* is a pure vowel pronounced with the lips rounded and slightly protruded)]

FRIEDA. No. I am an American. And I speak only English.

EMIL. Very wise. We will speak English. Also, I am glad to see you are correctly suspicious of me, because you think I am a child. But you can trust me. We will work together to defeat the enemy.

FRIEDA. You are insane.

EMIL. (*A childish note in his voice*) Please—don't try to deceive me. I have been informed. There are eight million of you in America—all good Germans—all working for *Der Führer* [/de[r] FÜ ruh/ (The Leader)]. Don't you understand? I know all about it. I am prepared.

FRIEDA. (*With sarcasm*) What are you prepared for? In your Nazi uniform!

EMIL. (*Re-assuming his air of authority*) You and I will have collaboration. We must find out everything. The Herr Professor is engaged in important work; I discovered that before I even left New York. We must examine all the letters; we must open all the telegraphs. Give me that telegraph.

(*He holds out his hand.*)

FRIEDA. You're also a fool.

4. From Arthur Miller's *After the Fall* (1964), Act 1

In this semi-autobiographical play, Helga (based on Miller's third wife, Austrian-born photographer Inge Morath, to whom the play is dedicated) talks to Quentin (the character who represents Miller) about her philosophy of life. Helga's Austrian accent is light: She speaks English very well.

HELGA. Quentin, I think it's a mistake to ever look for hope outside one's self. One day the house smells of fresh bread, the next of smoke and blood. One day you faint because the gardener cut his finger off, within a week you're climbing over the corpses of children bombed in a subway. What hope can there be if that is so? I tried to die near the end of the war. [. . .] The same dream returned each night until I dared not go to sleep and grew quite ill. I dreamed I had a child, and even in the dream I saw it was my life, and it was an idiot, and I ran away. But it always crept onto my lap again, clutched at my clothes. Until I thought, if I could kiss it, whatever in it was my own, perhaps I could sleep. And I bent to its broken face, and it was horrible . . . but I kissed it. I think one must finally take one's life in one's arms, Quentin. Come, they play *The Magic Flute* tonight. You like *The Magic Flute*?

4
Italian Accents

Approximately seventy-three million people speak Italian—an Indo-European language of the Romance family, descended from Latin—and its dialects. In Italy, widely varying dialects of Italian coexist with the Standard Italian that is taught in schools nationwide, as well as to foreigners learning the language all over the world. It is used in government, writing, and the media, but in practice there is no absolute standard spoken language even in the media, any more than there is a standard accent. As Anna Laura and Giulio Lepschy point out in *The Italian Language Today* (Ivan R. Dee, 1998), "Educated pronunciation is not uniform, but varies locally," as do vocabulary and grammar.

The major dialect families are:

1. **Northern:** These dialects include those of Venice and the Veneto, Lombardy, and Liguria.
2. **Tuscan:** Three groups: Western (Lucca), Central (Florence), and Southern (Siena).
3. **Central:** Northern Latium, including Rome.
4. **Southern:** These groups include Neapolitan, Calabrian, and Sicilian.

The dialects of the Italian language condition the accent in English as well as in Standard Italian itself: Neapolitan or Sicilian accents, for instance, are very different from Roman, Venetian, or Florentine pronunciations.

As Mario Rossi tells us in "Intonation in Italian," in *Intonation Systems* (Cambridge University Press, 1998), the dialect of Firenze /fih REN tse/ (Florence), "stripped of the characteristics which are specific to Tuscan dialects," among them Florentine intonation, became the de facto Standard Italian in writing, and eventually in speaking. This was partly because of the power of the Medici /ME di*h* chee/ dynasty, well established in the fourteenth century, and because it was the language of some of the greatest early Italian literature (of which there is an example in the quotation from Dante in the practice exercises). By the seventeenth century, it was also the standard accessible language of musical terminology and opera libretti. Performed all over Italy, opera was the popular music of its day, and in the nineteenth century everybody knew the operas of Rossini, Donizetti, and Bellini, as well as Verdi's political, patriotic works. The language of Florence was, thus, eminently suitable as a standard that everybody could learn while continuing to speak his or her own dialect.

See the charming film *Used People* (1992), with Marcello Mastroianni and Shirley MacLaine. The film is set in New York, and is good not only for Mastroianni's Italian accent, but for New York accents as well. Sophia Loren, in her many films, and Anna Magnani in *The Rose Tattoo* (1955) are worth listening to for their accents, quite aside from their superb performances. This is also the case with Eduardo Ciannelli in his Hollywood films, such as his first, *Reunion in Vienna* (1933), and his last American film, *The Secret of Santa Vittoria* (1969). See *Tea with Mussolini* (1999), about the expatriate British community in Florence, for the Italian accents of some of its characters, as well as for the English accents of Maggie Smith, Joan Plowright, and Judi Dench.

To hear Italian, see Federico Fellini's films, as well as Vittorio De Sica's moving account of Italian Jews during World War II, *Il giardino dei Finzi Contini* /ihl jahr DEE no DEee FIH*N* dzee kon TEE nee/ (*The Garden of the Finzi-Continis*; 1970). Ettore Scola's /ET to re SKO la/ *Una giornata particolare* /OOH nah jawr NAH tah pahr TIH ko LAH re/ (*A Special Day*; 1977), starring Sophia Loren and Marcello Mastroianni, is set in Italy in 1938, and portrays the situation of homosexuals under fascism.

Roles requiring an Italian accent include the headwaiter Luigi in Sir Arthur Wing Pinero's rarely revived *The "Mind the Paint" Girl* (1912), and the two Venetian gondoliers in Pinero's *The Notorious Mrs. Ebbsmith* (1896), who have to speak Italian. Tony, an Italian immigrant vintner in California, is one of the central characters in Sidney Howard's *They Knew What They Wanted* (1924), musicalized by Frank Loesser as *The Most Happy Fella* (1956). The story of Arthur Miller's *A View from the Bridge* (1955) centers on Eddie Carbone, his wife, Beatrice, and her cousins Marco and Rodolpho. Tennessee Williams's *The Rose Tattoo* (1950) is the saga of the unhappy marriage of Serafina Delle Rose, one of several Italian characters. Among other roles are Filippo Fiorentino in Elmer Rice's *Street Scene* (1929), Paravicini in Agatha Christie's *The Mousetrap* (1952), Mr. Patumiera in Israel Horovitz's *The Primary English Class* (1976), and Tito and Maria Merelli in Ken Ludwig's hilarious *Lend Me a Tenor* (1985).

Teach Yourself Italian Accents

1. **Positioning, placement, and use of the muscles of the mouth during speech:** The Standard Italian language, and Italian accents in English, feel as if they generally resonate just in front of the middle of the mouth. The tongue is held up, and its tip is often just where the gum ridge begins to curve up into the palate. The lips are slightly forward. The mouth opening is medium narrow much of the time.

2. **The sounds of /r/:** The trilled /r/ is the one used in Italian. It is given one trill or flap, except when doubled orthographically, and then it is pronounced twice, i.e., with two trills. (See the introduction for tips on how to pronounce a trilled /r/.) In a heavy Italian accent in English, use a trilled /r/ with one flap. In a lighter accent, use the

trilled /r/ only at the beginning of a syllable in the middle of a word like *very*; do a retroflex /r/ elsewhere.

3. **Vowels and diphthongs:** The Italian system of pure vowels is as follows: /ah/, spelled "a"; /e/, spelled "e"; the intermediate front vowel /*ih*/, spelled "i"; /o/, spelled "o"; and /ooh/, spelled "u." Each has two sounds: open and closed. This means, quite literally, that the mouth is either slightly more open or more closed when pronouncing the vowel. There is no schwa /uh/ in Italian, and every vowel, short or long, stressed or unstressed, is given its full value. Be careful when practicing Italian not to diphthongize the vowels: in other words, do not relax the jaw or glide the tongue when pronouncing them. Record yourself, and listen carefully for any hint of diphthongs. Listen to Italian opera singers and you will hear that they sing the same vowel for the duration of a coloratura passage. Giving vowels a full value in unstressed syllables carries over into an Italian accent in English.

   a. **Lengthened vowels:** In stressed syllables, lengthen vowels preceding /l/, /m/, /n/, and /r/. This gives the accent a characteristic rhythm.

   b. **Insertion of the schwa /uh/ or /ah/ between consonants in consonant clusters:** For phonetic comfort, in all Italian accents in English, a very brief schwa is often inserted between consonants where the combination does not exist in Italian: *that's right* /DAT suh RIT (alternatively, in Southern Italian accents, AT suh RIT)/, *in the front of the mouth* /*ih*n d*ih* FRONT o vuh d*ih* MOWT/, *sometimes more, sometimes less* /SO muh TIMZ MAWR (alternatively, MO) SO muh TIM zuh LES/. (Caveat: This is stereotypical and must be carefully and judiciously used, so that it is absolutely real; it is generally avoided in educated speech.) The insertion of /uh/ happens because in Italian the vast majority of syllables end in a vowel. There are short monosyllabic words that end in consonants. These words are simple grammatical words, such as *non* /NON/ (not), *il* /IHL/ (the masculine definite article "the"), and *con* /KON/ (with).

There are a limited number of consonant clusters in Italian. It is uncomfortable for many Italians, regardless of their specific dialect background, to pronounce the clusters in English that do not exist in Italian. The insertion of a schwa /uh/ is, therefore, very common in Northern Italian accents in English when one word ends in a consonant and the next word begins with a consonant. There are certain combinations of consonants that exist in Italian in the middle of a word and that would, therefore, be comfortable for an Italian to pronounce in English. Examples of this would include the /st/ in *pasta*, and in the initial position, such as /sm/, /sp/, and /st/; so the words *smile*, *sport*, and *state* would present no difficulty to a native Italian speaker learning English. The same is true of the consonants that go with /l/, such as the /pl/ in *place* and the /sl/ in *slow*: they exist in both English and Italian, and, therefore, present no difficulty to the Italian student of English. There is no insertion of a schwa between the consonants in these clusters.

In some cases in a Southern Italian accent you would hear /ah/ inserted instead of /uh/.

c. **The sound of /a/:** This sound does not exist in Italian. Substitute /ah/ or /e/ for the sound of /a/ in *that*.

d. **The sound of the intermediate front vowel /ih/:** The vowel /ih/ does not exist in Italian, and the usual substitutions for it are /ee/ or /ih/, with the tongue and mouth opening between that for /ee/ and /ih/.

e **The sound of /oh/:** Substitute the monophthongs (pure vowels) /aw/ or /o/ for the diphthong /oh/.

f. **The sound of /u/:** This sound does not exist in Italian. Substitute /ah/ for /u/: *but* /BAHT/, *love* /LAHV/.

g. **Italian diphthongs:** Every letter in an Italian word is pronounced. Diphthongs are spelled out in two letters, and each letter is more distinctly and separately pronounced than in an English diphthong: "ei" /ay (Eee)/, "ai" /I (AHee)/, "au" /ow (AHooh)/, "oi" /oy (AWee)/, "uo" /wo (oohO)/, "iu" /yooh (eeOOH)/, "ie" /ye (eeE)/. This phonetic characteristic can carry over into an Italian accent in English, with a precise pronunciation of both halves of a diphthong.

4. **Other consonants:** The Italian repertory of consonants is the same as in English, with the exception of /h/ and /th / th/, which do not exist in Italian. Although /zh/ does not exist in Standard Italian, it does in dialects such as Venetian, and is usually correctly learned. Consonants in Italian are softer than their English counterparts, but still clearly articulated. Double consonants are both pronounced, which has the effect when heard of lengthening the vowel, as in the name *Giovanni* /jo VAHN nee/. In an Italian accent in English, words with double consonants are spoken with a lengthened vowel: *matter* /MAHT ter/. Except for the consonants /g/ and /k/, there are no guttural sounds in Standard Italian.

a. **The silent /h/:** There is no /h/ sound in Italian, although the letter "h" is used in orthography. When a word begins with "h," the "h" is not pronounced: *ho* /O/ ([I] have). In an Italian accent in English, the initial /h/ is usually dropped, although it may be inserted where it does not normally exist: *how are you?* /OW ahr YOOH/, but *what hour is it?* /waht HOW uhr *ih* zeet/; [*h*]*all the time* /HAWL (alternatively, HAW luh) duh TIM/.

Important for the correct pronunciation of Italian names, phrases, and words: In Italian spelling, if "h" follows "c," "g," or "sc" /sh/ before "i" or "e," it makes those consonants hard: *cucchiaio* /kooh KYAH yo/ (spoon), *ghianda* /GYAHN dah/ (acorn), *che* /ke/ (which, that), *schiena* /SKYE nah/ (back). When "h" is not inserted before "e" or "i," the sounds of "c," "g," and "sc" are soft /ch/, /j/, and /sh/: *cileggio* /chih LEJ jo/ (cherry), *Luciano* /looh

CHAH no/, *Gemigniano* /je mih NYAH no/, *scena* /SIIE nah/ (stage, scene), *scimunito* /shih mooh NEE to/ (fool, rascal).

b. **The sound of /l/:** The Italian /l/ is produced by the tip of the tongue lightly touching the upper gum ridge just inside the opening upward into the palate. It resonates where the front vowel /ih/ does. This /l/ is often heard in an Italian accent in English.

c. **Substitutions for /th / th/:** Substitute /d/ for /th/ and /t/ for /th/.

d. **The sound of /w/:** This semi-vowel exists in Italian in the diphthong spelled "ua" as in *uguale* /ooh GWAH le/ (equal), "ue" as in *questo* /KWE sto/ (this), "ui" as in *Guido* /GWEE do/, or "uo" as in *buono* /BWO no/ (good), so there is no problem for Italians in pronouncing it correctly at the beginning of such words as *what*, *where*, *will*, or *won't*.

e. **Dropping of word endings:** In a Southern Italian / Sicilian accent, word endings are sometimes dropped, as they are in the original Italian dialect: *provolone* (a cheese): in Standard Italian /pro vo LO ne/; in Southern Italian / Sicilian /pro vo LON/. Entire word endings are sometimes dropped. My father had a friend from southern Italy who used to go into the woods to gather oak mushroom, an edible tree fungus, which he called /HOH ke MAHSH/.

For a light accent, keep the general positioning of the mouth muscles consistent during speech, using the Italian position when speaking English. Lengthen vowels in stressed syllables more than native English speakers do, and use some of the intonation patterns discussed below.

Intonation and Stress: The Music and Rhythm of the Accents

Stress in Italian is most often on the penultimate syllable. Accent marks in Italian indicate an unusual stress, but not a change in sound: *città* /chih TAH/ (city).

In Italian all unstressed vowels are short. All stressed vowels are long, especially the final stressed vowel of an utterance. Importantly, this characteristic is transferred into an Italian accent in English. There is, thus, a kind of rhythmic phrasing, created by the lengthening of stressed vowels and diphthongs, particularly the final stressed vowel; the stressed half of a diphthong is longer than in an accent native to English.

In non-regional Standard Italian intonation patterns, the pitch is usually high on stressed syllables, low on unstressed syllables. In a declarative sentence the pitch starts low, then rises, then falls again to end a sentence. In a question, the pitch rises at the end, but it may also fall, and the latter pattern is sometimes transferred to an Italian accent in English. In a command, the pitch starts high, then gradually falls to the end.

Practice Exercises
Practice in Italian

1. *Buon giorno. Come stà? Molto bene, grazie. E lei?* [formal "you"]
/bwon JOR no / KO me STAH / MOL to BE ne GRAH tsye / e LEee/

Literal translation: Good day. How stand [you]? Very well, thanks. And you?
Translation: Hello. How are you? Very well, thanks. And you?

2. From Dante Alighieri's /DAHN te ah lih GYE ree/ *La Divina Comme-dia* /lah dee VEE nah kom ME dee ah/ (*The Divine Comedy*; 1308–1321): *Inferno* /ihn FER no/ (Hell), Canto III /KAHN to TRE/: The Inscription on the Gates of Hell

Dante's (1265–1321) three-part allegorical epic poem about the journey of the soul from the darkness of *Inferno* through *Purgatorio* /POOR gah TO ree o/ (Purgatory) to the enlightenment of *Paradiso* /PAH rah DEE zo/ (Heaven, or Paradise) was written between 1308 and 1321.

> "Per me si va nella città dolente,
>   per me si va nell'eterno dolore,
>   per me si va tra la perduta gente.

Giustizia mosse il mio alto Fattore;
  fecemi la divina Potestate,
  la somma Sapienza e il primo Amore.

Dinanzi a me non fur cose create
  se non eterne, ed io eterno duro.
  Lasciate ogni speranza, voi ch'entrate."

/per ME see VAH NEL lah chih TAH do LEN te / per ME see VAH NEL le
TER no do LO re / per ME si VAH trah lah per DOOH tah JEN te/

/jooh STEE tsee ah MOS se ihl MEE o AHL to faht TO re / FE che mee lah
dee VEE nah po tes TAH te / lah SOM mah sah pee EN tsah e ihl PREE
mo ah MO re/

/dee NAHN tsee ah ME non FOOHR KO ze kre AH te / se non e TER ne ed EE
o e TER no DOOH ro / lah SHAH te O nyee spe RAN tsah VOY ken TRAH te/

Literal translation:
"Through me oneself goes into the city sorrowful [pain-filled; suffer-
ing], / through me oneself goes into eternal sorrow [suffering], / through
me oneself goes among the lost people.

Justice moved [motivated] the my high Maker; / made me the divine
Power, / the supreme Wisdom, and the first [primal] Love.

Before to me not were things created / if not eternal, and I eternal
last. / Abandon [Leave] all hope, you who enter."

Practice in English

3. *You got to exercise or it's no good. You get home, you sit in your chair, especially
in the wintertime. And we had a rough winter so far.*

Southern / Sicilian: /yooh GAH duh EK suh SIZ aw *rih* tsuh naw goohd / yooh ga dohm / yooh *SIH dih* nuh yooh CHE es PE shuh lee *ih* nuh W*IH*N tuh TIM / an wee a duh RAH fuh W*IH*N tuh saw FAH/

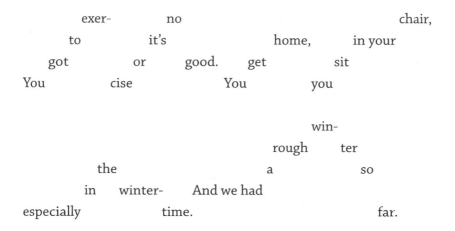

Notes: The /d/ sounds in the syllables /duh/, /dohm/, and /d*ih*/ are tapped. Lengthen the final vowels in the stressed syllables at the ends of phrases more than for native English speech.

4. *Italian cuisine is the world's greatest. It's real comfort food, you know? A plate of pasta with a great sauce, some meatballs, and you feel all's right with the world.*

/*IH* tahl yahn kwee ZEEN *ihz* dee WAWRL dzuh GRE test / *IH* tsuh R*IH*L KAHM for tuh FOOHD yooh NAW / uh PLAY dah vuh PAH stah wee duh uh GRAY duh SOHS sahm M*IH* tuh BAWLZ / en yooh F*IH*L AWL zuh RI tuh w*ih* duh WAWRL duh/

A Monologue and Three Scenes

1. From Tennessee Williams's *The Rose Tattoo* (1950), Act 1, Scene 1

Williams informs us that "the locale of the play is a village populated mostly by Sicilians somewhere on the Gulf Coast between New Orleans and Mobile." Married to truck driver Rosario Delle Rose /ro ZAH ree o

DEL le RO ze/, Serafina /se rah FEE nah/ (played by Anna Magnani in the 1955 film) eagerly awaits his return home, as she tells her neighbor Assunta /ahs SOON tah/. You can treat this brief scene as a monologue, ignoring Assunta's lines.

SERAFINA. On top of the truck is bananas! But underneath— something else!
[ASSUNTA. Che altre cose? [/ke AHL tre ko ze/ (What else?; literally, What other things?)]]
SERAFINA. Whatever it is that the Brothers Romano want hauled out of the state, he hauls it for them, underneath the bananas! (*She nods her head importantly.*) And money, he gets so much it spills from his pockets! Soon I don't have to make dresses!
[ASSUNTA. (*Turning away.*) Soon I think you will have to make a black veil!]
SERAFINA. Tonight is the last time he does it! Tomorrow he quits hauling stuff for the Brothers Romano! He pays for the 10-ton truck and works for himself. We live with dignity in America, then! Own truck! Own house! And in the house will be everything electric! Stove—deep freeze—*tutto!* [/TOOHT to/ (everything)]— But tonight, stay with me . . . I can't swallow my heart!—Not till I hear the truck stop in front of the house and his key in the lock of the door!—When I call him, and him shouting back, "*Si, sono qui!*" [/SEE SO no KWEE/ (Yes, I am here)] In his hair, Assunta, he has—oil of roses. And when I wake up at night—the air—the dark room's—full of—roses . . . Each time is the first time with him. Time doesn't pass . . .

2. Two Scenes from Arthur Miller's *A View from the Bridge: A Play in Two Acts* (1955), Act 1

The setting is Red Hook in Brooklyn, New York. Eddie Carbone is a long-shoreman unhappily married to Beatrice. Her cousins, brothers Marco

/MAHR ko/ and Rodolpho /ro DOL fo/, both illegal immigrants, have come from Italy and will be staying with the family. Marco falls in love with Eddie and Beatrice's niece, Catherine, whom the couple has raised since childhood. This situation arouses Eddie's bitter jealousy. He has been unconsciously in love with Catherine, and cannot admit it to himself, and he turns Marco and Rodolpho over to the immigration authorities.

In Sidney Lumet's 1962 film, Raf Vallone /RAHF vahl LO ne/, from Calabria, plays Eddie. Maureen Stapleton, from Troy, New York, is Beatrice, and speaks with a General American accent.

A. Eddie and Beatrice discuss the imminent arrival of her cousins.

BEATRICE. I'm just afraid if it don't turn out good you'll be mad at me.

EDDIE. Listen, if everybody keeps his mouth shut, nothin' can happen. They'll pay for their board.

BEATRICE. Oh, I told them.

EDDIE. Then what the hell. (*Pause. He moves.*) It's an honor, B. I mean it. I was just thinkin' before, comin' home, suppose my father didn't come to this country, and I was starvin' like them over there . . . and I had people in America could keep me a couple of months? The man would be honored to lend me a place to sleep.

B. Rodolpho and Marco, who have just arrived and are sitting with the Carbones at the dining room table, should have fairly heavy Italian accents. In Lumet's film, Raymond Pellegrin played Marco, and Jean Sorel played Rodolpho. Both actors are actually French, from Nice and Marseille, respectively; but they speak fluent Italian and also act in Italian films.

RODOLPHO. In harvest time we work in the fields . . . if there is work. Anything.

EDDIE. Still bad there, heh?

MARCO. Bad, yes.

RODOLPHO. (*Laughing*) It's terrible! We stand around all day in the piazza listening to the fountain like birds. Everybody waits only for the train.

BEATRICE. What's on the train?

RODOLPHO. Nothing. But if there are many passengers and you're lucky you make a few lire [/LEE re/] to push the taxi up the hill.

    (*Enter* CATHERINE; *she listens.*)

BEATRICE. You gotta push a taxi?

RODOLPHO. (*Laughing*) Oh, sure! It's a feature in our town. The horses in our town are skinnier than goats. So if there are too many passengers we help to push the carriages up to the hotel. (*He laughs.*) In our town the horses are only for show.

3. From Ken Ludwig's *Lend Me a Tenor* (1985), Act 1, Scene 1

In 1934, the Cleveland Grand Opera Company has eagerly awaited the famous Italian tenor Tito Merelli /TEE to me REL lee/, who, having over-eaten, is not feeling too well. His wife, Maria, is none too sympathetic, since she had told him not to indulge himself. Max and Saunders, already frazzled, are two of the people involved in arranging Tito's appearance at the opera.

MAX. Mr. Merelli?

SAUNDERS. Are you all right?

TITO. Me? I'm a-fine. *Perfetto*. [/per FET to/ (perfect)]

MARIA. (*Derisively*) Hoo!

TITO. I'm a-okey-dokey. I feel like ten bucks.

MARIA. Look at 'Im, eh? He looks a-like a sick dog.

TITO. I'm tip a-top.

MARIA. Liar!

TITO. Shut up!

MARIA. Phh!

TITO. A little stomach. It's nothing. I'm a-fine. A few more minutes, I'm gonna be even better.

SAUNDERS. Better?

MARIA. That's what I thought. I'll get a-you pills.

   (*She gets up.*)

TITO. (*A familiar argument*) I done take pills.

MARIA. You need a-pills!

TITO. No! I'm a-Merelli! Merelli says a-no!

MARIA. What's a-matter? You got a girl in there?

TITO. Yeah. Sure. I got a girl. I got two girls. Both a-naked. Go ahead! Look!

MARIA. Some day, you gonna wake up in a-you bed, you gonna be a soprano!

TITO. (*To* MAX) Jealousy, eh? Jealousy! It's a-terrible.

MARIA. (*Overlapping, to* SAUNDERS) In my heart, he makes a-me sick.

TITO. (*Overlapping*) She's a crazy woman.

MARIA. (*Overlapping*) Because he's a-stupid. He's got a-no brains.

TITO. (*Overlapping*) All the time it's a-jealousy, jealousy, jealousy—

MARIA. SHUT UP!

TITO. SHUT UP A-YOUSELF!

5
Russian Accents

Russian, an Indo-European language of the Slavic (also called Slavonic) family, is spoken by some 215 million people in Russia, of whom about 61 million speak it as their second language. Although the pronunciation of educated speakers is fairly uniform throughout the vast country, Russian does have three main accent areas: Northern, Southern, and Central, which includes Moscow.

For examples of Russian accents listen to Michael Chekhov, a great actor, acting teacher and theorist, and the playwright Anton Chekhov's nephew, as the psychiatrist in Hitchcock's *Spellbound* (1945); Maria Ouspenskaya in *The Wolf Man* (1941) and many other films; Rudolf Nureyev in *Valentino* (1977); Mikhail Baryshnikov in *White Nights* (1985); and Yul Brynner in *The King and I* (1956). Vladimir Sokoloff and Akim Tamiroff (who, like Michael Chekhov and Ouspenskaya, studied with Stanislavsky at the Moscow Art Theatre) appear in dozens of Hollywood films: See them in *For Whom the Bell Tolls* (1943), and see Tamiroff in is his Oscar-nominated performance in *The General Died at Dawn* (1936), and Sokoloff in *The Magnificent Seven* (1960), with Yul Brynner. Mischa Auer, from St. Petersburg, worked extensively in French and American films; watch him in *My Man Godfrey* (1936) and *Sweethearts* (1938). Appearing in more than a hundred films and television shows, Leonid Kinskey, also from St. Petersburg, plays Sascha, the bartender at Rick's, in *Casablanca* (1942). Although primarily a stage actress, Moscow-born Eugenie Leontovich made several television programs and films, including *The World in His Arms* (1952) and *The Rains of Ranchipur* (1955). She married Gregory Ratoff, from St. Petersburg; he made fifty films and television shows, and appears as the producer Max Fabian in *All About Eve* (1950). To hear Russian spoken, see the classic sound films of Sergei Eisenstein.

Roles requiring Russian accents include the King of Navarre and his nobles, who disguise themselves as Russians to visit the Princess of France and her ladies in Shakespeare's *Love's Labour's Lost* (1594–1595)—see also chapter 6; the dance instructor Kolenkhov and the Grand Duchess Olga Katrina in Kaufman and Hart's madcap farce *You Can't Take It With You* (1936); Count Paul Vasilich Vronoff in Elmer Rice's *Flight to the West* (1940); Colonel Ikonenko in Peter Ustinov's satirical *The Love of Four Colonels* (1951); the Russian ambassador and his wife and son, as well as a spy, in Ustinov's *Romanoff and Juliet* (1956); and Kerner, a Russian double agent and scientist residing in London in Tom Stoppard's *Hapgood* (1995). In Elena Miramova and Eugenie Leontovich's Broadway play *Dark Eyes: A Comedy in Two Acts* (1943), there are several Russian characters, including Natasha Rapakovich, played by Leontovich herself. In Lee Blessing's two-character Pulitzer Prize– and Tony Award–winning Broadway play, *A Walk in the Woods* (1988), Andrey Botvinnik is a professional Soviet arms negotiator.

Teach Yourself Russian Accents

1. **Positioning, placement, and use of the muscles of the mouth during speech:** The Russian language and Russian accents in English feel as if they resonate generally just forward of the middle of the mouth. The tongue is forward and held up toward the roof of the mouth. The lips are slightly forward, and relaxed at the corners. The mouth opening is medium wide much of the time.

2. **The sounds of /r/:** There are two rhotic sounds in Russian:

a. **The trilled /r/:** This /r/ is given one trill or flap. In a medium or heavy Russian accent in English, use the trilled /r/ at the beginning of a word or syllable, especially in the middle of a word, such as *very* /VE (alternatively, VA) ree/, with the stressed vowel being of sustained duration. See the introduction for tips on how to pronounce the trilled /r/.

b. **The retroflex /r/:** This /r/ is similar to the one heard in English. The retroflex /r/ is, therefore, easy for Russians to use, especially after a vowel.

3. **Vowels and diphthongs:** The Russian vowel inventory is much the same as in English, with the exceptions noted below. Russian vowels have short and long versions, depending on whether they are stressed or unstressed, and this idea often carries over into a Russian accent in English. Vowels are often lengthened before /r/. The diphthongs formed with /y/ exist in Russian, so there is no problem pronouncing them in English.

a. **The shift from /a/ to /e/:** There is no /a/ sound in Russian, and /e/ is often substituted for /a/ in a Russian accent in English: *that* /DET/. But /a/ is sometimes learned, and substituted for /e/: *debt* /DAT/, instead of being correctly used in words like *that*.

b. **The sounds of /e/, /ye/, and /a/:** The letter "E," "e" in lowercase, in the Cyrillic alphabet represents the diphthong, or palatalized semi-vowel, /ye/ as in *yes*. This is the sound one sometimes hears in words like *that* in a heavy Russian accent: /DYET/ or even /DYETS/, with the /t/ dentalized. But /e/ may also be correctly pronounced, or in a heavy accent shifted to /a/: *let* /LAT/, *Let's go* /LYETS GAW/ or /LATS GAW/.

c. **The sounds of /ee/, /ih/, and the intermediate front vowel /ih/:** The sound of /ih/ in *bit* does not exist in Russian. Substitute the intermediate front vowel /ih/, with the tongue and mouth opening between that for /ee/ and /ih/; or /ee/, which you should also use for words containing the vowel /ee/. As an alternative, pronounce words with /ee/ with the intermediate front vowel /ih/.

d. **The sound of /o/:** This sound does not exist in Russian, and /aw/ or /e/ is substituted for it: *first* /FAWRST/ or /FERST/, *work* /VAWRK/ or /VERK/.

e. **The shift from /oh/ to /aw/:** In words with the diphthong /oh/, such as *home*, shift the diphthong to the vowel /aw/: /KHAWM/. The diphthong /oh/ does not exist in Russian.

f. **The shift from /u/ to /ah/:** The sound /u/ does not exist in Russian. Instead, Russians substitute the vowel /ah/: *but* /BAHT/, *love* /LAHV/.

4. **Other consonants:** The Russian inventory of consonants is the same as in English, with the exception of /h/ and /th / th/, which do not exist in Russian. The consonants have hard and soft versions, both of which are softer than the English ones. The soft versions, with less pressure of the articulators (lips, tongue) on each other than in the hard versions, are pronounced with the lips slightly parted. The soft version is always the one heard when the consonant is palatalized.

a. **Palatalization of consonants:** Certain consonants occurring before /e/ and /ih/ in Russian are palatalized, including /ch/, /d/, /l/, /p/, /t/, /ts/, /zh/, and the nasal consonants /m/ and /n/. This means that the tongue touches the roof of the mouth just after the pronunciation of the consonant, resulting in the insertion of the semi-vowel /y/ between the consonant and the following /ih/ or /e/: *nyet* /NYET/ (no), *nichevo* /NYIH chye VAW/ (nothing). These consonants are articulated with the tongue near the hard upper palate, with a "glide" into the semi-vowel /y/. This feature of the language can carry over into English, particularly in a heavy accent: *I read the article* /I RAD vee AHR tyih (alternatively, chih) kuhl/. Words like *duke* and *newspaper* are easy to say in their palatalized versions: /DYOOHK/, /NYOOHZ PAY puhr/.

b. **Occasional dentalization of /d/ and /t/:** When palatalized before /e/ and /*ih*/ in Russian, /d/ and /t/ are pronounced with the tongue farther forward behind the upper front teeth than are the English versions, resulting, when this is carried over into English, in dentalization: *dinner* /DZIH (alternatively, DZY*IH*) ner/, *tea* /TSEE/. This characteristic must be used judiciously and without exaggerating the dentalization.

c. **The shift from /h/ to /kh/:** There is no /h/ sound in Russian. The name of Shakespeare's play is *Gamlet* /GAHM lyet/ in Russian. Substitute a soft /kh/ if your character has not learned to pronounce /h/.

d. **The sounds of /l/:** There are two Russian /l/ sounds:
   1. **The light /l/:** In the formation of this /l/, the tongue is tensed and its tip pressed against the back of the upper front teeth. The semi-vowel /y/ is formed just after this /l/ when pronounced before /*ih*/ or /*e*/: *let* /LYET/ (flight; Cyrillic spelling: LET). It resonates where the back vowel /o/ does.
   2. **The dark, palatalized /l/:** In the formation of this /l/, much of the tongue, including its middle, is raised to touch the roof of the mouth, creating a deep opening at the back. This /l/ is often heard in a Russian accent in English. This palatalized /l/ resonates where the back vowel /e/ resonates.

e. **The substitutes for /th / th/:** Substitute /d/ and /t/ or /v/ and /f/ for /th / th/: *this thing* /DIHS TIHNG/ or /VIHS FIHNG/.

f. **The shift from /w/ to /v/:** Substitute /v/ for initial /w/, or pronounce /w/ correctly, if your character has learned English well: *what* /VAHT/, *where* /VER/, *when* /VEN/. Sometimes, although initial /v/ exists in Russian, there is an overcompensatory tendency to substitute an initial /w/ for it in a very heavy Russian accent: *very* /WE ree/.

g. **Consonant clusters:** Many consonants in Russian come together in clusters. Such consonant clusters as occur regularly in English, therefore, present no problems to the Russian speaker learning English. There are consonant clusters in Russian that do not exist in English, such as /shch/ as in the name *Khrushchev* /khroohsh CHAWF/. The only time this combination occurs in English is between two words: *rush chair, flush cheek.*

h. **Devoiced final consonants:** In English, the consonants spelled "d," "s," and "v" are pronounced /d/, /z/, and /v/ at the end of a word, but these same sounds are voiceless in Russian: /t/, /s/, and /f/, and this phonetic characteristic carries over into an accent in English: *end* /ENT/, *is* /IHS/, *Romanov* /rah MAH nof/ (the czar's family name; sometimes anglicized as /ROH muh NAWF/).

For a light accent, keep the general positioning of the mouth muscles consistent during speech, using the Russian position when speaking English. Do /r/ and /th / *th*/ sounds correctly, and follow the advice under intonation and stress, particularly lengthening stressed vowels slightly beyond the normal English duration.

For a heavier accent, do the vowel and diphthong substitutions, and add to this the substitution of /kh/ for /h/ and substitutions for /th / *th*/.

For a really heavy accent, add to this the full use of palatalization.

The Pronunciation of Russian Names

It is easy to learn to read the Cyrillic alphabet in which Russian is written, a necessity if you have to learn the accurate pronunciation of Russian names, because the transliteration of Cyrillic letters into the Roman alphabet is often problematic. The Cyrillic letter "Є" and lower-case "є" stand for the sound /e/, and are transliterated as "e." But although the Cyrillic letters "E" and lowercase "e" stand for the diphthong /ye/, they are usually also transliterated as "e." The Cyrillic letters "Ё" and lowercase "ё" are usually transliterated as "e" as well, even though they stand for the diphthong /yaw/; often, however, "ё" is transliterated, accurately, as "yo": *Fedor, Feodor,* or *Fyodor* (Theodore), all three transliterations pronounced /FYO dor/.

Russians have three names: a first name, a patronymic, and a last name.
The second name, the patronymic, is the name of the person's father with
a masculine or feminine ending, indicating that the person is his son or
daughter. The ending is never stressed: instead the patronymic receives the
stress of the root name; for example, *Stepan Stepanovich* /styih PAHN styih
PAHN uh vihch (alternatively, styih PAHN ihch)/ (Stephen, son of Stephen);
the feminine patronymic is *Stepanovna* /styih PAHN uhv nah/ (daughter of
Stephen). The "ov" in a man's patronymic is often not pronounced, but the
patronymic derived from *Pyotr* (Peter), with its stress on the "o," stresses
the second syllable of the patronymic: *Petrovich* /pyih TRO vihch/ (son of
Peter), *Petrovna* /pyih TROV nah/ (daughter of Peter). *Ivan Aleksandrovich*
can be pronounced either /ee VAHN ah lyihk SAHN dro vihch/ or /ee VAHN
ah lyihk SAHN drihch/ (John, son of Alexander); *Aleksandrovna* /ah lyihk
SAHN drov nah/ is the feminine patronymic. *Ivan Ivanovich* is usually pronounced /ee VAHN ee VAHN nihch/. *Ilya*, which, in Russian, is stressed on
the last syllable, /eel YAH/, also stresses the patronymic on the last syllable,
so the name of the character known as "Waffles" (Russian, *Vaflya* /VAH fl
yah/) in *Uncle Vanya*, Ilya Ilyich Telyegin, is pronounced /ee LYAH ee LYIHCH
tye LYE gihn/; the first syllable of the last name is anglicized to /te/.

The diminutive endings indicating endearment, which abound in Russian
novels and plays, are not stressed. For example, Mashenka /MAH shuhn
kah/—used by the old nurse Anfisa /ahn FEE sah/ in Chekhov's *Three Sis-
ters*—is the diminutive of Masha /MAH shah/, itself a diminutive of Maria.
It is not pronounced, as I have heard it in productions, /mah SHEN kuh/.

You can look up the correct pronunciation of Russian last names in Morton Benson's eminently useful *Dictionary of Russian Personal Names with
a Guide to Stress and Morphology* (University of Pennsylvania Press, 1967).
The names are all in the Cyrillic alphabet, with stress clearly indicated.

Intonation and Stress: The Music and Rhythm of the Accents

Stress patterns in Russian, like those in English, are random; that is, the
stress could be on any syllable in a word, and you have to learn each one.

Russians usually encounter no difficulty in learning to stress English words correctly.

One phenomenon that gives a Russian accent its characteristic rhythm is that long vowels in stressed syllables tend to be really long; conversely, short vowels in unstressed syllables are really short. Before /r/, vowels are often lengthened.

Intonation patterns are similar to English, with lengthened stressed syllables spoken on a differentiated pitch, often a higher one than a native English speaker would use. One Russian intonation pattern that is transferred into an accent in English consists of a continuous rise throughout a declarative sentence until the end, spoken on a falling tone. In a question there is sometimes a falling tone at the end, where we would use a rising tone in English.

Practice Exercises
Practice in Russian
Note: I have transliterated these exercises from the Cyrillic alphabet.

1. *Ztravstfuitye. Kak vui pozhivaete? Khorosho, spasebo. I vui?* [formal "you"] /STRAHST fwee tye / KAHK vwee PAH zh*ih* VAH y*ih* ty*ih* / KHAH rah SHAW SPAH see buh / ee VWEE/

Literal translation: Hello. How you on-living (alternatively, on-getting [with life])? Good, thanks. And you?
Translation: Hello. How are you? Well, thanks. And you?

Note: The diphthong in the Russian word *vui* does not exist in English, and must be heard by a native speaker to reproduce it accurately. Another way of writing the pronunciation: /VOOHee/.

2. From Anton Chekhov's /AHN ton CHYE khof/ ДЯДЯ ВаНЯ /DYAH dyah VAHN yah/ (*Dyadya Vanya* [*Uncle Vanya*]; 1897), Act 1

Written by Anton Chekhov (1860–1904) in 1897, *Uncle Vanya*, first pre-
sented at the Moscow Art Theatre in 1899, takes place on a rural estate
during a hot summer. Ivan Ivanovich Voinitsky /ee VAHN ee VAHN o
*vih*ch voy NY*IH*T skee/, known as Uncle Vanya, has fallen in love with
Yelena Andreevna /*yih* LYE nah ahn DRYE yev nah/ (usually anglicized
in American and U.K. productions to /ye [alternatively, e] LAY nah
ahn DRAY yev nah/), the wife of his former brother-in-law, Professor
Serebriakov /sye rye bree ah KOF/, who now owns the estate that belonged to his dead first wife, Vanya's sister. At the end of act 1, when
Vanya and Yelena are alone, he finally works up the courage to tell her
how he feels.

> YELENA ANDREEVNA. Veroyatno, Ivan Pyetrovich, ottovo mui
> c vami druz'ya, shto oba mui nudn'ye skuchn'ye lyudi! Nudn'ye!
> Nye smotritye na myenya tak, ya etovo nye lyublyu.
> VOINITSKY. Mogu li ya smotryet' na vas inachye, yesli ya lyublyu
> vas? Vui moye schast'ye, zhizn', moya molodost'!

/*yih* LYE nah ahn DRYE yev nah / ver o YAHT no ee VAHN p*yih* TRO
*vih*ch / ah tah VO MWEE SVAH mee DROOZ yah / shto O bah MWEE
NOOD nye SKOOCH nye LYOOH dee / NOOD nye / n*yih* smah TREE tye
nah m*yih* NYAH TAHK / yah E to vo NY*IH* lyooh BLYOOH/
/voy NY*IH*T skee / mah GOO lee yah smah TRYET nah VAHS ee NAH
chye / YES lee yah lyooh BLYOOH VAHS / vwee MAH ye SCHAHS
tye / ZH*IH*ZN / MAH yah MAH lah DOST/

Literal translation:
YELENA ANDREEVNA. Truthfully, Ivan Petrovich, why I and you friends,
that both we [both of us are] bothersome, boring people! Bothersome! Not
look at me so, I that not like. [Don't look at me like that. I don't like it.]
VOINITSKY. Can I look at you otherwise, if I love you? You [are] my hap-
piness, life, my youth!

Practice in English

3. *Well, you know, they call Little Odessa out here in Brighton Beach, because of large Russian population.*

/vel yuh NAW vay KAWL L*IH* tuhl ah DYE suh owt KHEE r*ih*n BRI tn B*IH*CH / b*ih* KAWZ ahv LAHRJ RAH shuhn pop yooh LAY shuhn/

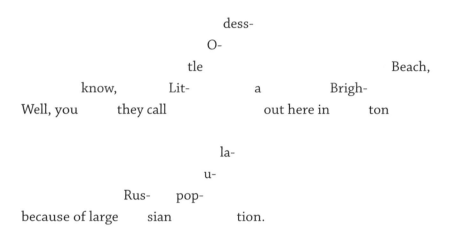

4. *Did you ever read Chekhov's short story "Lady with Lapdog," but, of course, that's really completely different, and it's take place in different kind of resort town.*

/d*ih*uhd yooh A vuh R*IH*D CHYE khuhfs SHAWRT STAW ree LE dee v*ih*f LEP dawg buh duhf KAWRS dets R*IH* lee kawm PL*IH* tlee DY*IH* frant (alternatively, fruhnt) en *ih*ts TEK PLES *ih*n DY*IH* frant KIN awf r*ih* ZAWR TAHN/

Three Scenes and a Monologue

1. Two Scenes from Kaufman and Hart's *You Can't Take It With You* (1936)

A. From act 2: In this riotous, complicated madcap farce, Boris Kolenkhov /bah REES ko lyen KOF/—anglicized as /BAW rihs kuh LEN kawf/, as in Frank Capra's 1938 film version—is a stereotypical Russian refugee from the 1917 Revolution, and staunchly Czarist in his political sympathies.

He has come to visit the eccentric, artsy, generous Vanderhof family, who
live near Columbia University and open a sympathetic door to everyone.

In the 1938 film, which won the Oscar for Best Picture, Grandpa is played
by Lionel Barrymore, and Kolenkhov by Mischa Auer.

> GRANDPA. How are you, Kolenkhov?
> KOLENKHOV. Magnificent! Life is chasing around inside of me,
> like a squirrel.
> GRANDPA. 'Tis, huh? . . . What's new in Russia? Any more letters
> from your friend in Moscow?
> KOLENKHOV. I have just heard from him. I saved for you the
> stamp. (*He hands it over*)
> GRANDPA. (*Receiving it with delight*) Thanks, Kolenkhov.
> KOLENKHOV. They have sent him to Siberia.
> GRANDPA. That so? How's he like it?
> KOLENKHOV. He has escaped. He has escaped and gone back to
> Moscow. He will get them yet, if they do not get him. The Soviet
> Government! I could take the whole Soviet Government and—
> grrah!

B. From act 3: Kolenkhov brings the Grand Duchess Olga Katrina, now a
waitress at Childs' (a popular, inexpensive restaurant chain), to dinner at
the Vanderhofs', since the poor lady is starving. She hopes soon to work
at Schraffts', a slightly classier establishment than Childs'. She mentions
Hattie Carnegie's, an exclusive high-end fashion store, and Kolenkhov
mentions Luna Park, an amusement theme park in Coney Island, Brooklyn.

This scene is not in the film, which is quite different in some ways from
the play, nor is the Grand Duchess a character in the movie.

> GRANDPA. Quite a lot of your family living over here now, aren't
> there?

THE GRAND DUCHESS. Oh, yes—many. My uncle, the Grand Duke Sergei—he is an elevator man at Macy's. A very nice man. Then there is my cousin, Prince Alexis. He will not speak to the rest of us because he works at Hattie Carnegie's. He has cards printed—Prince Alexis of Hattie Carnegie. Bah!

KOLENKHOV. When he was selling Eskimo Pies at Luna Park he was willing to talk to you.

THE GRAND DUCHESS. Ah, Kolenkhov, our time is coming. My sister Natasha is studying to be a manicure. Uncle Sergei they have promised to make floor-walker, and next month I get transferred to the Fifth Avenue Childs'. From there it is only a step to Schraffts', and *then* we will see what Prince Alexis says!

2. From Peter Ustinov's *Romanoff and Juliet: A Comedy in Three Acts* (1956), Act 1

In this satire on Shakespeare's play and the politics of the Cold War era, Igor Romanoff /EE gawr ROH muh NAWF/, the son of the Soviet ambassador, and Juliet Moulsworth, the daughter of the American ambassador to the "smallest country in Europe," fall in love and decide that love can overcome politics. Here, Vadim /vah DEEM/ and Evdokia /yev DO kee ah/ Romanoff remonstrate with their son. They all have Russian accents, each one different. Igor, the romantic lead, has the lightest accent. There is also a Russian spy hiding in the room in the Soviet Embassy where the scene takes place, spying on them for the government.

IGOR. I am in love.

EVDOKIA. A fine time you choose, I must say, with Junior Captain Marfa Vassilievna Zlotochienko arriving today. [/MAHR fah vah *SIHL* yev nah ZLAH tah CHYEN ko/]

IGOR. With who arriving?

EVDOKIA. Your betrothed. The heroic commander of the sloop *Dostoievsky*.

IGOR. My betrothed? But I've never even heard of her.

ROMANOFF. We intended to introduce her to you before the marriage.

IGOR. I should hope so.

ROMANOFF. Don't be ridiculous, and start behaving like a spoiled child. I met your mother for the first time at our wedding. There was no time for surprise. We were both spared the degradation of emotional behavior.

IGOR. I refuse to marry this female!

EVDOKIA. You will do as you're told! We have noted with considerable regret that you are prone to unstable and introspective behavior, and that at times you are as self-pitying as a fascist.

ROMANOFF. Evdokia, you are going too far.

EVDOKIA. Yes, and I know where he gets it from. Talking in your sleep about imperial occasions in St. Petersburg. St. Petersburg, if you please, not even Petrograd.

SPY. Most interesting. [. . .]

ROMANOFF. (*Roused*) And what about you? Yesterday, when I took you shopping, you lingered for a full quarter of an hour outside a shop displaying French hats.

SPY. Oh—ho!

EVDOKIA. (*Uncertain*) I did it to pour my scorn on them.

3. From Lee Blessing's *A Walk in the Woods* (1988), Act 1, Scene 2

In the Cold War era, John Honeyman, "an American negotiator," and Andrey Botvinnik /ahn DRAY BOT vy*ih* ny*ih*k (Anglicization, BOT vih nihk)/, "a career Soviet negotiator" who has "a very slight accent," meet in "a pleasant woods on the outskirts of Geneva" to try to accomplish something away from the negotiating table. They discuss the situations of their two countries, and many other political issues of the day.

The published version names the character Joan Honeyman. In a 2011 British production, Joan was performed by Miriam Cyr, with Steven

Crossley as Botvinnik. In the Broadway production, Robert Prosky did a brilliant, light accent as Botvinnik. Honeyman was played by Sam Waterston. You can see a brief excerpt on the Acorn Media DVD *The Best of the Tony Awards: The Plays* (2005). Treat this excerpt as a monologue; Honeyman's lines in brackets are there simply for continuity.

BOTVINNIK. I hear certain words—whether I say them or someone else says them—words like "détente," "human rights," "Star Wars," "Central America," "readiness," "early warning," and I feel like I am falling away from the Earth. I can see the Earth—the entire planet, like I am a cosmonaut. And it is falling away from me. We are both simply—receding into the dark. Sometimes I spend entire conversations in this kind of darkness, while I am hearing words like "summit," "test ban," "emigration," "strategic objectives." It is almost as though the words are printed . . . on the dark walls . . . all around me. And the Earth is by then like a . . . fingertip, it is so far away. (*A beat.*) Does this ever happen to you? [HONEYMAN. No.]

BOTVINNIK. Perhaps it will someday. In any case, you must forgive me. This does not happen at the table. There, I listen very carefully. There I pretend we are discussing a different planet from Earth, and that helps very much.

[HONEYMAN. Andrey . . .]

BOTVINNIK. Receptions, dinner parties—that's where it happens. I hear all those serious words: "lasers," "megadeaths," "acceptable losses". . . Do you know what I am dying to hear an American talk about? Mickey Mouse. Cowboys. How to make a banjo.

6

Spanish Accents

Spanish—an Indo-European language of the Romance family, descended from Latin—is spoken as a first language by four to five hundred million people. It is the principal language of Spain, with its provincial, urban, and classical Castilian dialects and accents; of most South American countries; of Mexico and the rest of Central America; and of many Caribbean islands, including Puerto Rico, Cuba, and Hispaniola, where the Dominican Republic is located.

All these variants ensure that, in practice, there is no standardized language or accent. Nevertheless, a dialect derived partly from Medieval Castilian Spanish, and called Standard or sometimes Neutral Spanish, with its formalized grammar and pronunciation, is studied by students and by foreigners learning the language. Widely spoken by educated people, Standard Spanish is also the language of literature and is used in film and the media.

For Spanish accents in English, listen to Antonio Banderas, from the province of Andalucía, in *Frida* (2002) and *The Legend of Zorro* (2005); to Penélope Cruz, from Madrid, in *Vanilla Sky* (2001) and *Sex and the City 2* (2010); to Javier Bardem, from the Canary Islands, in *No Country for Old Men* (2007) and *Skyfall* (2012); and to Spanish-American comedienne Charo, from Murcia, Spain, in *Moon over Parador* (1988) and her many television appearances. For Hispanic accents of the Americas, listen to Dolores Del Rio, Carlos Santana, Salma Hayek, and Ricardo Montalban—all from Mexico—in their many films; and to Desi Arnaz and Oscar Nuñez, both from Cuba. Gael García Bernal, from Mexico, speaks perfect English, with just a touch of his Mexican Spanish accent; see him in *Y Tu Mamá También* /ee tooh mah MAH tahm BYEN/ (*And Your Mama Too*; 2001), *The Motorcycle Diaries* (2004), and *Letters to Juliet* (2010).

To hear the Spanish of Spain, see the films of Pedro Almodóvar /PE dro ahl mo DO vahr/, including *La mala educación* /lah MAH lah e dooh KAH thee YON (South American, see YON)/ (*Bad Education*; 2004), starring Gael García Bernal; and *Volver* /vol VER/ (Return; 2006)—pronounced with the soft Spanish /v/ that sounds very like /b/—starring Penélope Cruz. And don't miss Guillermo del Toro's powerful *El laberinto del fauno* /el lah be RIHN to del FOW no/ (*Pan's Labyrinth*; 2006), set in Fascist Spain in 1944.

Roles in plays and musicals that require Spanish accents include the Castilian Don Armado in Shakespeare's *Love's Labour's Lost* (1594–1595), Queen Katherine of Aragon in William Shakespeare and John Fletcher's *All Is True* (commonly known as *The Famous Life of King Henry the Eighth*; 1613), and the Spanish bandit chief Mendoza in George Bernard Shaw's *Man and Superman* (1903). Anita and other characters in *West Side Story* (play, 1957; film, 1961) are Puerto Rican, and *In the Heights* (2007), by actor-composer Lin-Manuel Miranda and Quiara Alegría Hudes, tells the story of Dominican-American characters. In the mordantly satirical, incisive plays of Luis Valdez about the Mexican-American experience, a number of characters require accents, among them those in his 1967 one-act play *Los vendidos* /los ven DEE dos/ (literally, The Sold [Ones]), in which Chicano English (ChcE) accents are used; and *Bandido!: The American Melodrama of Tiburcio Vásquez, Notorious California Bandit* (1981) /bahn DEE do; tee BOOR syo VAHS kes/, in which Tiburcio Vásquez, with a light Mexican Spanish accent, is the principal character. In José Rivera's *The House of Ramon Iglesia* /rah MON ih GLE syah/ (1983), Ramon Iglesia and his wife, Dolores, have Puerto Rican Spanish accents, as does Paco in Miguel Piñero's searing prison drama *Short Eyes* (1974). And there are roles requiring Spanish accents in the brilliantly crafted, riveting plays of Cuban-Americans

Nilo Cruz and Maria Irene Fornes. The characters in the satirical comedies of the group Latins Anonymous, *Latins Anonymous* (1989) and *The LA LA Awards* (1993), speak with various Hispanic accents.

Teach Yourself Spanish Accents

The main accent covered here is Castilian, and there are also some details on South American accents. For information on Chicano English (ChcE), a dialect with its own grammatical features and vocabulary, and other Hispanic accents in the United States, see *Teach Yourself Accents—North America*.

1. **Positioning, placement, and use of the muscles of the mouth during speech:** The Spanish language, and Spanish accents in English, feel as though they resonate generally near the front of the mouth. The tongue is held fairly low, with its tip raised slightly. The lips are relaxed. They touch lightly to articulate such consonants as /b/ and /v/. The mouth opening is medium wide much of the time.

2. **The sounds of /r/:** The /r/ in Spanish is softly trilled, usually receiving one tap, or, if doubled orthographically, two taps. See the introduction for tips on how to pronounce a trilled /r/, which you often hear in Castilian Spanish accents in English.

    a. **The retroflex /r/:** Many speakers learn the retroflex /r/, and pronounce it with the back of the tongue tensed slightly, the tip retracted as it curls upward, the sides of the tongue pressed lightly against the sides of the palate, and the lips slightly protruded. Since post-vocalic (after a vowel) /r/ is pronounced in Spanish, a General American accent may sometimes come easier to Spanish speakers than British RP.

3. **Vowels and diphthongs:** The vowel system in Spanish consists of /ah/, spelled "a"; /e/, spelled "e"; the intermediate front vowel /ih/,

spelled "i"; /o/, spelled "o"; and /ooh/, spelled "u." The vowels have open and closed versions. Vowels, particularly in final syllables, are lengthened slightly, and the duration of the syllable is sustained. Diphthongs often shift to pure vowels in a Spanish accent in English. Diphthongs formed with /w/ and /y/ exist in Spanish, but have various pronunciations in English, indicated below.

   a. **The sounds of /ee/, /ih/, and /ih/:** Substitute a lengthened /ee/ for both /ih/, which does not exist in Spanish, and /ee/. You may also substitute the intermediate front vowel /ih/, with the tongue and mouth opening between those for /ee/ and /ih/.

   b. **The shift of /oh/ to /aw/:** In a heavy Spanish accent, /oh/ shifts to a short /aw/, so *home* is pronounced /KHAWM/.

   c. **The sound of /u/:** This sound does not exist in Spanish. Substitute /ah/ for /u/ in such words as *but* and *love*.

   d. **The sound of /w/:** In Spanish, /w/ exists initially and after some consonants: *huevos* /WE vos/ (eggs), *bueno* /BWE no/ (good). In a Castilian Spanish accent in English, /w/ is occasionally preceded in some words by a soft /kh/: *what* /KHWAHT/, with a very soft, sometimes nonexistent /t/; *where* /KHWER/.

   e. **The sounds of /y/:** This semi-vowel has various pronunciations in Spanish, which carry over into English. In Castilian, /y/ is like its English counterpart. In Argentina it sounds like /zh/, and in Puerto Rico and Cuba almost like the /j/ in *edge*. *Yo no se* (I don't know) is /yo no SE/ (Castilian), /zho no SE/ (Argentina), and /jo no SE/ (Puerto Rico). In Chicano English and Salvadoran accents, initial /y/ is pronounced somewhat like /ch/: *you* /CHOOH/. The way the /y/ sound is pronounced in Spanish is often the way it is pronounced in English in heavy accents.

4. **Other consonants:** The Spanish inventory of consonants is the same as in English, with the exception of /h/, /j/, /th/, /z/, and /zh/ (heard in some dialects), which do not exist in Spanish. Consonants are well articulated, and softer than in General American. Keep the

lips slightly parted when articulating bilabial consonants, such as /b/ and /v/, which sound like each other in Spanish itself.

a. **The sounds of the letter "c":** In Spanish orthography, the letter "c" is pronounced /k/ before the letters "a," "o," and "u." Before the letters "e" and "i," "c" is pronounced /*th*/ in Castilian, and /s/ in Central and South America, and in the Caribbean. In a heavy Castilian accent in English, use the /*th*/ sound for /s/ at the end of a word or syllable; otherwise use /s/.

b. **The sound of /ch/:** The consonant /ch/ exists in Spanish, but usually only initially, so final /ch/ is sometimes heard as /sh/: *church* /CHORSH/.

c. **The tapped /d/:** The tapped /d/, in which the tongue does not press strongly against the back of the gum ridge to form a hard /d/, is heard not only at the beginning of a syllable in the middle of a word (see below under /th / *th*/) but also in consonant clusters, as in the word *didn't* /DIH dihnt/, where the tapped /d/ at the beginning of the second syllable is very lightly articulated. The General American pronunciation is /DIH dnt/, with only the slightest hint of a schwa between /d/ and /n/. A glottal stop may substitute for the final /t/; sometimes the final /t/ is dropped altogether, especially before another consonant: *I didn't know* /I DIH dih (alternatively, DIH ?ih) NOH/ (often heard in New York City).

d. **The sound of /h/:** Although the letter "h" is used in Spanish orthography, the sound of /h/ does not exist in Spanish pronunciation, but the letters "j" and "x" are used to represent a soft /kh/. Substitute a soft /kh/ for initial pronounced /h/ in a Spanish accent in English.

e. **The shift from /j/ to /ch/:** The /j/ sound does not exist in Spanish, and /ch/ is often substituted for it, especially in Castilian, Salvadoran, and Chicano English: *edge* /ECH/, *stranger* /STREN chuhr/.

f. **The Spanish /l/:** The Spanish /l/ is pronounced with the tip of the tongue forward, just behind where the upper gum ridge opens up into the palate. It resonates where the front vowel /ih/ does. This sound is also heard in a Spanish accent in English.

g. **The sounds of /n/ and /ng/:** The /n/ at the end of a word is often heard as /ng/ in some accents of the Spanish language, particularly in Cuba and Puerto Rico. Sometimes the vowel preceding the letter "n" is nasalized. The word *ten* in the Cuban or Puerto Rican accent in English of someone whose first language is Spanish is heard variously as /TENG/ or /TEN/, with the /e/ nasalized.

h. **The sounds of /sh/ and /zh/:** Voiceless /sh/ often substitutes for the voiced /zh/, which does not exist in Spanish except in some dialects, so that *measure*, for example, is pronounced /MAY shuhr/, especially in a heavy Castilian Spanish accent.

i. **The sounds of /th / th/:** Substitute /d/ and /t/ for /th/ and /th/, and a tapped /d/ for /th/ and for /t/ when the sounds occur between vowels: *other* /U duhr/, *matter* /MA duhr/. But /th/, which exists in Castilian Spanish and is used for the letters "c" before "e" and "i" and for the letter "z," is often correctly pronounced, especially by educated speakers, as is /th/, since the soft Spanish /d/ is close to the sound of /th/.

j. **The devoicing of /z/ to /s/ and the sounds of /s/:** There is no voiced /z/ sound in Spanish, although the letter is used in spelling. The usual substitution in a Spanish accent in English is /s/. In South America the letter "z" is pronounced /s/, and in Castilian Spanish, /th/. But even in a Castilian accent in English, /s/ is substituted for /z/. Do not exaggerate this characteristic: Pronounce /s/ lightly, without dwelling on it, particularly at the end of a word where the sound is often spelled with an "s": *please* /PLEES/, *says* /SES/, *does* /DOS/. In South American Spanish, there are accents in which all final /s/ sounds, spelled "s," as well as /s/ sounds before another consonant are dropped, as are many final consonants: *muchas gracias* (many thanks) /MOOH chahs GRAH thee ahs/ in Castilian; /MOOH chah GRAH see ah/ in Puerto Rican, Canary Islands, and some South American varieties of Spanish. An initial /s/ does not exist in Spanish when /s/ is followed by another consonant; instead it is preceded by /e/, which is heard in a Spanish accent in English: *España* /e SPAH nyah/ (Spain), *español* /e spah NYOL/ (Spanish). Notice that the unstressed syllables retain the full value of the vowel and are not reduced to a schwa. Pronouncing English words beginning with /s/ followed by another consonant as if they began with /es/ gives a characteristic, if clichéd, touch to a Spanish accent in English: *he's stupid* /khees e STOOH pihd/ (*estúpido* /e STOOH pee do/ in Spanish). Occasionally the /s/ is pronounced as a retroflex consonant, with the bottom of the tongue turned toward the roof of the mouth.

k. **Consonant cluster reduction:** Drop the final /d/ or /t/ in consonant clusters in words like *old*, *fast*, *last*, and *most*.

For a light accent, keep the general positioning of the mouth muscles consistent during speech, using the Spanish position when speaking English. Substitute /s/ for /z/ sounds. Add to this some of the Spanish intonation patterns discussed below.

For a heavier accent, add to this the substitution of /kh/ for /h/.

Intonation and Stress: The Music and Rhythm of the Accents

Almost every word in the Spanish language is stressed on the penultimate (next to last) syllable, unless the word ends in a consonant, and in that case the last syllable is stressed. Accent marks in Spanish indicate that a syllable outside those rules is stressed. In other words, the stress for the purposes of an actor wanting to do a Spanish accent in English is random enough so that there is usually no problem for Spanish-speaking people in learning to stress English words correctly. We have to look to phonetics and pitch patterns, which are different for each variety, for the characteristics that create a Spanish accent in English.

The following general patterns are often transferred to a Castilian Spanish accent in English: Stressed syllables are spoken on an upper pitch, higher than that of English. The pitch falls at the end of a simple declarative sentence. The last stressed syllable in an utterance is spoken on a lower pitch than the earlier stressed syllables.

Practice Exercises
Practice in Spanish

1. *Buenos días. ¿Como estás? Muy bien, gracias. ¿Y tu?* [informal "you"]
/BWE nos DEE ahs / KO mo es TAHS / MOOHee BYEN GRAH *thee* ahs / ee TOOH/

Literal translation: Good days. How are you? Very well, thanks. And you?
Translation: Hello. How are you? Very well, thanks. And you?

2. From *El ingenioso hidalgo Don Quijote de la Mancha* /el *ihn* khe nee O so ee DAHL go don kee KHO te de lah MAHN chah/ (*The Ingenious Gentleman Don Quixote de la Mancha*; 1605 and 1615) by Miguel de Cervantes Saavedra /mee GEL de ser VAHN tes (Castilian pronunciation, *ther* VAHN tes) sah VE drah/, Capítulo primero /kah PEE tooh lo pree ME ro/ (Chapter 1)

Published in 1605 and 1615, this picaresque, ironic, sentimental novel by Cervantes (1547–1616) concerns the wanderings of the nobly idealistic yet delusional Don Quixote, in love with chivalry and romance.

> En un lugar de la Mancha, de cuyo nombre no quiero acordarme, no ha mucho tiempo que vivía un hidalgo de los de lanza en astillero, adárga antigua, rocín flaco y galgo corredor.

/en oohn looh GAHR de lah MAHN chah de KOOH yo NOM bre no KYE ro ah kor DAHR me no ah MOOH cho TYEM po ke vee VEE ah oohn ee

DAHL go de los de LAHN *th*ah (alternatively, LAHN sah) en ahs tee YE ro
ah DAHR gah ahn TEE gwah ro *TH*EEN (alternatively, ro SEEN) FLAH ko
ee GAHL go kor re DAWR/

Literal translation: In a place [village] of la Mancha [an area south of Castile
and just west of Valencia] of which the-name not desire-I to-remember-
to-myself, not has-been much time [not long ago] that lived a gentleman
of those of lance in rack, shield antique, nag skinny [lanky; scrawny] and
greyhound for-run [chase; hunt].

Note: All the consonants are softer than their English counterparts, so
that /v/ is almost like /b/, /d/ like /th/, and so on.

Practice in English
3. *For this cake the fruit is marinating in liquor and it is absorbing the rum.*
/fawr dees KAYK dee FROOH *ih*s (alternatively, d*ih*s) MAH ree NAY deeng
*ih*n LIH kor an *ih* dees ah SAWR veeng dee ROM/

			mar-					
			na-					
	fruit	i-	ting	li-		sor-		
cake		is		in	quor		bing	rum.
For this	the				and ab-		the	

Notes: The /d/ sounds in the syllables /d*ih*s/, /deeng/, and /dees/ are
tapped. Notice the /v/ substitute for /b/ in the word "absorbing."

4. *I drive him in my taxi to 345 Houston Street. It's very far over. He gets out,
and he's off.*
/I DRI kheem een mI TAH see tyooh *TH*REE FAWR dee FI KHOW sten
STREE / ees BE ree fah ROH vah / khee GES ow en khee SAWF/

```
                tax-       345
   drive              i       Hous-
I        him              to         ton
          in my                    Street.


       ve-
         ry    o-          out,
It's      far        gets     and he's
          ver. He                off.
```

Notes: A New York taxi driver from Spain said this to me, complaining that his passenger hadn't paid him. Note the two different pronunciations of "v" in *very* and *over*, and the dropping of the final /v/ in *five*. The syllables /KHOW/ and /ROH/ are very long, giving the sentences their particular rhythm. Also notice the linking of final consonants, such as /s/ in *he's*, to the following word, *off*. Note, too, the correct pronunciation of /th/ in *three*. As I heard it, /kh/ for /h/ in *him* was softer than /kh/ in *Houston*, which was quite a hard sound. And notice the insertion of /y/ in the word *to*.

Four Monologues

1. From William Shakespeare's *Love's Labour's Lost* (1594–1595), Act 1, Scene 2

In this romantic comedy, the "fantastical Spaniard" Don Adriano de Armado /DON ah dree AH no de ahr MAH do/ falls madly in love with the peasant wench Jaquenetta, and does not like this fact, for he has sworn an oath to abstain from love and to spend three years in studying and learning, along with the King of Navarre and several of his courtiers, for whom he is the "keeper" or chaperone. The King of Navarre describes Armado, who "haunts" his court, as "a refined traveler of Spain; / A man in all the world's new fashion planted, / That hath a mint of phrases in his brain."

Armado should have a heavy Spanish accent: no /z/ sound, but only /s/; /kh/ substituted for the letter "h"; and a voiceless /th/ pronounced wherever the letter combination "th" occurs. Drop the final /d/ in *ground* in line 1, the final /d/ in *guided* in line 2, the final /t/ in *that* in line 4, the final /d/ in *hard* in line 8, the final /d/ in *Spaniard's* and the final /t/ in *first* in line 9, and the final /t/ in *not* in line 10; and make all final consonants very soft. Pronounce *respects* and *regards* in lines 10 and 11 as /ree SPEKS/ and /ree GAHRS/. In line 14, pronounce *extemporal* as /es TEM po rahl/. In line 4, pronounce *attempted* either as /ah TEN teth/ or /ah TENK ted/; the soft Spanish /d/ is close to the English voiced /th/. Do not trill all the /r/ sounds: Pronounce a retroflex /r/ in most places, with the back and sides of the tongue slightly tensed and the tip of the tongue fairly far back. Here is a suggested pronunciation for the last line: /dee VIS weet RI pen faw RI yam fawr KHOL VOL yoohms een FAW lyo/—make all final consonants in this line very soft.

ARMADO. I do affect the very ground, which is base, where her shoe,
which is baser, guided by her foot, which is basest, doth tread.
I shall be forsworn,—which is a great argument of falsehood,—if
I love. And how can that be true love which is falsely attempted?
5 Love is a familiar; Love is a devil; there is no evil angel but
Love. Yet was Samson so tempted, and he had an excellent
strength; yet was Solomon so seduced, and he had a very good wit.
Cupid's butt-shaft is too hard for Hercules' club, and therefore
too much odds for a Spaniard's rapier. The first and second cause
10 will not serve my turn; the passado he respects not, the duello
he regards not; his disgrace is to be called boy, but his glory
is to subdue men. Adieu, valour! rust, rapier! be still, drum!
for your manager is in love; yea, he loveth. Assist me, some
extemporal god of rime, for I am sure I shall turn sonneter.
15 Devise, wit; write, pen; for I am for whole volumes in folio.

2. From William Shakespeare and John Fletcher's *All Is True* (commonly known as *The Famous Life of King Henry the Eighth*; 1613), Act 1, Scene 4
Henry VIII has decided to divorce his wife of more than twenty years, "Queen Katherine, later Katherine, Princess Dowager," in order to marry Anne Boleyn. Katherine should have a light accent: Substitute a soft /kh/ for /h/, /s/ for /z/ sounds, and /sh/ for /zh/.

> QUEEN KATHERINE. Sir, I desire you do me right and justice,
> And to bestow your pity on me; for
> I am a most poor woman, and a stranger,
> Born out of your dominions, having here
> No judge indifferent, nor no more assurance
> Of equal friendship and proceeding. Alas, sir,
> In what have I offended you? What cause
> Hath my behavior given to your displeasure,
> That thus you should proceed to put me off
> And take your good grace from me? Heaven witness,
> I have been to you a true and humble wife,
> At all times to your will conformable;
> Ever in fear to kindle your dislike,
> Yea, subject to your countenance, glad or sorry
> As I saw it inclined. When was the hour
> I ever contradicted your desire,
> Or made it not mine too? Or which of your friends
> Have I not strove to love, although I knew
> He were mine enemy? What friend of mine
> That had to him derived your anger, did I
> Continue in my liking? nay, gave notice
> He was from thence discharged? Sir, call to mind
> That I have been your wife in this obedience
> Upward of twenty years, and have been blest
> With many children by you. If, in the course

And process of this time, you can report,

And prove it too, against mine honour aught,

My bond to wedlock, or my love and duty,

Against your sacred person, in God's name,

Turn me away; and let the foul'st contempt

Shut door upon me, and so give me up

To the sharp'st kind of justice. Please you, sir,

The King, your father, was reputed for

A prince most prudent, of an excellent

And unmatched wit and judgment; Ferdinand,

My father, King of Spain, was reckoned one

The wisest prince that there had reigned by many

A year before; it is not to be questioned

That they had gathered a wise council to them

Of every realm, that did debate this business,

Who deemed our marriage lawful; wherefore I humbly

Beseech you, sir, to spare me till I may

Be by my friends in Spain advised, whose counsel

I will implore. If not, i' the name of God,

Your pleasure be fulfilled!

3. From George Bernard Shaw's *Man and Superman: A Comedy and a Philosophy* (1903), Act 3

In this tale about the battle of the sexes and male chauvinism, the English-man Jack Tanner, who is Shaw's Don Juan figure, and his chauffeur, Henry Straker, are taken prisoner by brigands while journeying in the mountains of Spain. The brigand chief is Mendoza, a Spanish Jew, and this is part of the conversation they have while sitting at night around a campfire.

Mendoza, who was once a waiter in a London restaurant, speaks English quite well, and should have a light Castilian accent. Straker has a London Cockney accent. You can treat this excerpt as a monologue, with Straker's lines lending it a sense of continuity.

MENDOZA. The woman I loved—

[STRAKER. Oh, this is a love story, is it? Right you are. Go on: I was only afraid you were going to talk about yourself.]

MENDOZA. Myself! I have thrown myself away for her sake: that is why I am here. No matter: I count the world well lost for her. She had, I pledge you my word, the most magnificent head of hair I ever saw. She had humor; she had intellect; she could cook to perfection; and her highly strung temperament made her uncertain, incalculable, variable, capricious, cruel, in a word, enchanting. [STRAKER. A six shillin novel sort o woman, all but the cookin. Er name was Lady Gladys Plantagenet, wasn't it?]

MENDOZA. No, sir: she was not an earl's daughter. Photography, reproduced by the half-tone process, has made me familiar with the appearance of the daughters of the English peerage; and I can honestly say that I would have sold the lot, faces, dowries, clothes, titles, and all, for a smile from this woman. Yet she was a woman of the people, a worker: otherwise—let me reciprocate your bluntness—I should have scorned her.

4. From *Latins Anonymous* (1989) by Latins Anonymous (Luisa Leschin, Armando Molina, Rick Nájera, Diane Rodríguez)

Latins Anonymous is a group of Hispanic-American actors and writers who decided in the late 1980s to write their own play, spoofing Latina / Latino stereotypes in Hollywood movies and the media, and in public perception—a project similar in theme to Luis Valdez's *I Don't Have to Show You No Stinking Badges!* (1986), in which Connie and Eddie play bit parts using stereotypical accents in order to put their children through college.

Lolana is a workout instructor, and is just finishing up a class.

LOLANA. (*Calling off-stage*) Good workout, girls! See you next week. Bye, Debbie, bye, Susie, bye, Buffy! (*To audience*) Ay, those *gringa* workouts, they want to lose ten pounds in one hour! *Hola, chicas*! [/O LAH CHEE kahs/ (Hello, girls!)] Welcome to Lolana aerobics! I'm Lolana and, ooh, I'm feeling good. Okay! (*She removes aerobic shoes and puts on spike heels in preparation for her class.*) This is the Advanced Latin Woman's Aerobics class where we exercise our femininity. And, *chicas*, don't let anybody kid you, femininity does not come natural, uh, uh, it takes technique! For today's class, our focus is going to be on . . . *men*! Oh, I like that! Okay! When you see a man you want, *chicas*, you've got to be like a heat-seeking missile. (*She picks a man and slinks over.*)

Hi. I know you're a man. Oh, I like that. Will you love Lolana? (*Pause.*) You see? Dead silence. Why? Because I'm using bad technique. You can't ask a man to love you, you've got to *inspire* him to love you. So, okay, *chicas*! Let's inspire! We're going to warm up our most lethal weapon . . . our hips! (*Shaking her hips like maracas*) A Latina's hips know no rest. They work twenty-four hours a day. Dusting. (*Sings Santana's "Oye como va"*) [/O ye KO mo VAH/ (Hi, how goes [it]?)] Standing still. *Amorcito*, [/ah mor SEE to/ (little love)] will you zip me up?

7
Swedish Accents

Swedish, descended from Old Norse, is an Indo-European language of the Nordic (North Germanic) group of the Germanic family, and the most widely spoken Scandinavian language. It is the native tongue of more than nine million people in Sweden, and of several hundred thousand people in Finland, which was once part of the Swedish kingdom. There are also pockets of native speakers in the United States, notably in northern Wisconsin and Minnesota.

Swedish has rural and provincial as well as Stockholm and other urban accents. The light Swedish accents of movie stars Greta Garbo and Ingrid Bergman, both from Stockholm, are excellent examples to study. They are characterized by an occasional slight over-articulation of devoiced final consonants (/s/ instead of /z/: *his* /HIHS/), and a Swedish lengthened "ø" sound—/o/—in such words as *work* and *first*. Max von Sydow, who has made so many films in both Swedish and English, has only the lightest occasional trace of a Swedish accent in his perfect English; but he can do a heavier accent, as he does in *The Emigrants* (1971) and its sequel *The New Land* (1972), about the struggles of pioneer Swedish farmers in Minnesota. The late Viveca Lindfors, who appeared in *The Way We Were* (1973) and *Stargate* (1994), also had a light Swedish accent. For the sound of Swedish itself, see the films of Ingmar Bergman.

Listen to the actors in the English-language version of *The Girl with the Dragon Tattoo* (2011) for the contemporary Swedish accents of some characters and actors, among them Stellan Skarsgård. He has a medium heavy accent, not characterized by the use of the Swedish tones. And see the 2009 Swedish version as well, *Män som hatar kvinnor* /MEN soom HAH tahr KV*IH*N\ nor/ (literally, Men Who Hate Women).

Roles requiring Swedish accents include Chris Christopherson and his daughter Anna in Eugene O'Neill's *Anna Christie* (1921), and Ole Olsen in O'Neill's one-act play *The Long Voyage Home* (1917). Adapted for the movies by John Ford in 1940 along with three other of O'Neill's "sea plays," *The Long Voyage Home* stars John Wayne as Olsen. His portrayal is sympathetic, but you can forget the accent, even though he studied it thoroughly. In Elmer Rice's *Street Scene* (1929) and in Kurt Weill's 1946 musical adaptation, with a book by Rice and lyrics by Langston Hughes, Carl and Olga Olsen are the Swedish immigrant janitor and his wife.

Other plays with Swedish characters include Carl M. Dalton's *Ole Olson in Spiritland* (1902), Lawrence Russell's *A Prince of Sweden* (1905), Charles A. Lindholm, Sr.'s *The Man from Minnesota* (1911), and Perley Henry Ames's *Ole, the Nonpartisan Leaguer* (1921). In the popular nineteenth-century melodrama *Tilly Olson*, the title character is a virtuous Swedish domestic on a farm in Minnesota who overcomes all odds, including a mustache-twirling villain, and marries the man she loves. A comic Swedish immigrant trilogy— *Ole Olson* (1889), *Yon Yonson* (1890), and *Yenuine Yentleman* (1895)—by the now-forgotten German-American playwright and actor Augustus "Gus" J. Heege was very popular in its day. Of German and Irish parentage, El Brendel /EL bren DEL/, born Elmer Brendel in Philadelphia, became famous in vaudeville for his shticky Swedish-accented character Ole, featured in comic two-reelers in the 1930s and '40s; you can see some of them on YouTube.

Teach Yourself Swedish Accents

Language teaching in Sweden and in all of Scandinavia is excellent. You will seldom hear a heavy accent of the kind described here, which is associated with the accents of immigrants to the United States in the early part of the twentieth century, like the characters in *Anna Christie*. Nevertheless, one or more of these phonetic traits can be heard in the accents of some people.

1. **Positioning, placement, and use of the muscles of the mouth during speech:** The Swedish language, and Swedish accents in English, feel as if they resonate generally toward the front of the mouth. The tongue is held fairly low. The lips are protruded slightly, but relaxed. The mouth opening is medium wide much of the time.

2. **The sounds of /r/:** A lightly trilled /r/ is used in Swedish. Use a trilled /r/ with one tap in a heavy Swedish accent in English. See the introduction for tips on how to pronounce a trilled /r/.

3. **Vowels and diphthongs:** The vowel inventory in Swedish is much the same as in English, with the exceptions noted below, and with the addition of /ü/, spelled "y" and sometimes "u."

   a. **The sound of /ih/:** The vowel /ih/ does not exist in Swedish, and the usual substitute for it is the intermediate front vowel /ih/, with the tongue and mouth opening between those for /ee/ and /ih/.

   b. **The sound of /ooh/:** The English vowel /ooh/ has no exact equivalent in Swedish, in which a similar vowel /ooh/ is spoken with the lips protruded and almost closed. The result in a heavy Swedish accent in English is that /ü/ or /yü/ is substituted for it in a heavy Swedish accent: *too much* /TYÜ MOCH/, *true* /TRÜ/.

   c. **The sound of /u/:** There is no exact equivalent in Swedish for the vowel in *love* and *but*, so the schwa /uh/, or the vowels /e/, /o/, or /ah/, are usual substitutions.

4. **Other consonants:** The Swedish inventory of consonants is the same as in English, with the exceptions noted here. Consonants are softer than their English counterparts. They present no particular problems to Swedish people learning English, with the following important exceptions:

a. **The shift from /j/ to /y/:** There is no /j/ in Swedish, and the usual stereotypical, but accurate, substitution is /y/. In a heavy accent, substitute /y/ for initial /j/ as in the word *just* /YOOST/, and /ch/ for the final /j/ as in the word *edge* /ECH/.

b. **The sounds of /kv/ and /kw/:** The sound combination /kw/, spelled "qu" in English, does not exist in Swedish, but the combination /kv/, spelled "qu" in Swedish, does exist, and is the usual substitution in a heavy Swedish accent in English: *queen* /KVEEN/.

c. **The sound of /l/:** The Swedish /l/ is light and forward, with the front part of the blade of the tongue touching the upper palate behind the gum ridge. It resonates where the front vowel /ih/ does.

d. **The sound of /s/:** The /s/ in Swedish is retroflex: /s/ is pronounced with the bottom of the tongue turned slightly toward the roof of the mouth. When preceded by the letter "r," the letter "s" at the end of a word is pronounced /sh/ in Swedish, but this does not carry over into an accent in English.

e. **The sound of /sw/:** The usual substitution for this sound, which does not exist in Swedish, is /sv/, which does exist in Swedish: *Sweden* /SVEE den/ (*Sverige* /SVER ye/ in Swedish).

f. **The sounds of /th / th/:** These sounds do not exist in Swedish. In a Swedish accent in English, /d/ and /t/ are often substituted for /th / th/, especially in the middle of a word: *other* /O duh/.

g. **The sounds of /v/ and /w/:** The semi-vowel /w/ does not exist in Swedish, and a soft /v/ is substituted for /w/: *what* /VAHT/.

For a light accent, keep the general positioning of the mouth muscles consistent during speech, using the Swedish position when speaking English. Lengthen /o/ sounds slightly, and make the /j/ sound, which does not exist in Swedish, soft, like all the consonants.

Intonation and Stress: The Music and Rhythm of the Accents

Stress in Swedish is random. Vowels in stressed syllables are of sustained duration, giving the language a characteristic rhythm. In Swedish and English stress patterns are similar: In both languages, longer sentences are automatically separated by the speaker into phrases in order to communicate information, and each phrase has its own pitch and stress patterns. These are flexible, but each word nevertheless retains its stress, and the most important word receives the greatest stress.

In English, the pitch of a tone (high, low, rising, or falling) has nothing to do with a word's dictionary meaning (as it does in such "tonal" languages as Mandarin Chinese), but rather with the speaker's feeling and intentions. While this is also true of Swedish, there are certain intonations that do change the lexical definition: The most noticeable intonational feature in Swedish is the use of two tones, or pitch accents, obligatory for certain words, on stressed syllables. The pitch accents are heavily or lightly done, and, depending on the speaker, they can be very lightly intoned indeed. These tonal patterns can carry over into a very heavy Swedish accent in English. The tones are absent in the pronunciation patterns of such celebrated screen stars as Max von Sydow, Stellan Skarsgård, Viveca Lindfors, Greta Garbo, and Ingrid Bergman.

1. **Accent One, also called Acute Accent:** A single falling tone that starts high and ends low. It can occur in any stressed syllable, including the last syllable of a word, or on a monosyllabic word. The vowel in the preceding syllable is lengthened slightly. The symbol used in this book for a falling tone is one backward slash (\).

2. **Accent Two, also called Grave Accent:** A double or compound falling tone, the first part of which starts high and falls slightly, the second of which rises a slight bit above the final fall of the first tone, and then falls again. The symbol used in this book for a compound tone is two backward slashes (\\).

Although Swedish is not a tonal language, it does contain about five hundred contrasting pairs of words that depend on one of the two accents for their meaning. For example, *fallet* /FAH let\/ (case; grammatical case), spoken on a single falling tone (Accent One in Swedish), changes its meaning when spoken on a double falling then rising tone (Accent Two in Swedish): *fallet* /FAH\\ let/ (fallen).

The first half of the tone is sustained or dwelt on for an instant, then falls abruptly, giving a very characteristic music in Swedish. It is this particular intonation that is heard in a heavy Swedish accent in English:

Jag var hem och såg glasena på bordet.
/ya vahr HEM\ ok saw GLAHS\ en ah paw BOOHR\\ det/

```
                              ena      bord-\\
             hem\                   på
Jag  var          och  såg  glas-\              et.
```

Translation: I was home and saw the [drinking] glasses on the table.

Practice Exercises
Practice in Swedish
1. *God dag. Hur står det till? Mycket bra, tack. Och Du?* [formal "you"]
/goo DAH / hür STOOHR de TIHL / MÜ ke BRAH\ TAHK / ok DÜ/

```
      dag.    r        till?       et br-\   tack.
God    Hu-                Myck-    a,              Du?
              står
                   det                      Och
```

Literal translation: Good day. How stands it to? Very good, thanks. And you?

Translation: Hello. How are you? Very well, thanks. And you?

Notes: The /d/ in *det* is tapped. The final /r/ sounds are very light, almost silent, and the vowels are r-influenced, as, for instance, in the word *Hur*. The "å" means that the vowel is pronounced sometimes /aw/, /o/, or, as here, /ooh/. Lengthen the stressed vowel in *Mycket*. Do not exaggerate Accent One in the word *bra*. Another phrase for "How are you?" is *Hur mår Du?* /hür MAWR DÜ/ (literally, How feel you?).

2. From August Strindberg's /OW goost STR*I*HN BER yuh/ one-act play *Fröken Julie: Ett Naturalistiskt Sorgespel* /FRO ken YOOH lee et NAH tooh rah L*I*HS tihskt SAWR ye SPEL/ (*Miss Julie: A Naturalistic Tragedy*; 1888)

The principal theme of this play by August Strindberg (1849–1912), written in 1888, is the way the battle of the sexes and the working of the class system intertwine and reinforce each other. In the summer of 1874, during the servants' ball on her father the Count's estate, the unmarried twenty-five-year-old Miss Julie flirts with the well-educated, ambitious, but servile Jean, who is thirty. Jean is the Count's manservant, and is engaged to the cook, Kristin, his elder by five years. Miss Julie wants to escape her hidebound life by running away with him. Jean has just entered the kitchen, where the play takes place. Here are the opening lines of the play.

> JEAN. I quäll är fröken Julie galen igen; komplett galen!
> KRISTIN. Så, är han här nu?
> JEAN. Jag följde grefven till station, och när jag kom tillbaka förbi logen, gick jag in och dansade, och så får jag se fröken anföra dansen med skogvaktarn.

/ZHAHN / ee KFEL er FRO ken YOOH lee GAH len ee YEN / kom PLET GAH len/

/KR*ih*S t*ih*n / SO er hahn HER nü/
/ZHAHN / yah FOL yde GREF en t*ih*l stah SHYON / ok ner yah kom t*ih*l
BAH kah FOR bee LO gen / Y*IH*K yah *ih*n ok DAHN sah de / ok so FOR
yah SE FRO ken ahn FO rah DAHN sen med SKO VAHK tahrn/

Literal translation:
JEAN. This evening is Miss Julie crazy again. Completely crazy!
KRISTIN. So, are you here now?
JEAN. I accompanied the Count to the station, and when I came to the
barn, went I in and danced, and so noticed I the Miss leading the dance
with the gamekeeper.

Practice in English
3. *If you have never tried a Swedish smörgåsbord, with its tempting array of
dishes, you are in for a real treat. Drottningholm is also worth a visit, with its
opera season and its real, eighteenth-century court theater, where you can see
a thunderstorm re-created as they saw it back then.*
/*ih*f yü haf NE vuhr (alternatively, fuhr) TRIT uh SVEE dihsh SMOR gos
BOOHuhR v*ih*t *ih*ts TEMP t*ih*ng a RAY *ov* D*IH* shuhs yü ahr *ih*n fawr ay
R*IH*L TREET\ / DROT n*ih*ng HOLM *ih*s AWL saw VORT ay V*IH* s*ih*t / v*ih*t
*ih*ts O pe rah SEE suhn an *ih*ts REEL AY teent SEN tyuh ree KAWRT TEE
uh tuhr / ver yü kan see uh TON der STAWRM ree kree AY ted es day SAW
*ih*t bak den/

4. *Do you care for music? In Sweden we have the most wonderful singers and
musicians, like the tenor Jussi Björling, whose voice was meltingly beautiful,
or the majestic Birgit Nilsson, quite incredible.*
/duh yü KAYR fawr MYÜ\ s*ih*k / *ih*n SVEE den vee haf dih mawst VON der
fool SIHNG uhs an MYÜ S*IH* shuhns lIk dih TE nuhr YOO see BYOR l*ih*ng
hooohs VOYS (alternatively, FOYS) vahs MELT *ih*ng lee BYÜ t*ih* fool / awr
dih mah YES\ t*ih*k B*IH*R y*ih*t N*IH*L\ suhn KFIT ihn KRED\\ *ih* bol/

Note: Pay attention to the lengthened vowels in such words as *meltingly* and *beautiful*. Like the tones with their lengthened vowels, they are a key to the rhythm of the accent.

Two Scenes and Two Monologues

The scenes and monologues that follow are from Eugene O'Neill's *Anna Christie: A Play in Four Acts* (1921), which won a Pulitzer Prize in 1922. The story, set in the year 1910, concerns Chris Christopherson, the Swedish captain of a coal barge and a perennial drunk, being reunited with his daughter Anna after a fifteen-year absence. During those years, Anna had lived with relatives in Minnesota. For part of that time she had been a prostitute, a fact that she conceals from her father. Anna falls in love with an Irish sailor, Matt Burke, and finally reveals her checkered past to both of them.

In the 1930 film, Greta Garbo plays Anna, and George F. Marion plays Chris Christopherson. The American characters are Matt Burke (Charles Bickford), Larry (Lee Phelps), and Marthy (Marie Dressler).

1. In the opening scene of act 1, Chris Christopherson, who has just received a letter from Anna, is in "Johnny-the-Priest's" saloon near the waterfront in New York City, his usual hangout, with his friends Larry the bartender and Marthy, who runs the place. As O'Neill shows us, the character has a very heavy accent, thickened no doubt by his drunken state.

> CHRIS. (*Pauses for a moment, after finishing the letter, as if to let the news sink in—then suddenly pounds his fist on the table with happy excitement*) Py yiminy! Yust tank, Anna say she's comin' here right avay! She gat sick on yob in St. Paul, she say. It's short letter, don't tal me much more'n dat. (*Beaming*) Py golly, dat's good news all at one time for ole fallar! (*Then turning to* MARTHY, *rather shame-facedly*) You know, Marthy, Ay've tole you Ay don't see my Anna since she vas little gel in Sveden five year ole.

MARTHY. How old'll she be now?

CHRIS. She must be—lat me see—she must be twenty year ole, py Yo!

LARRY. (*Surprised*) You've not seen her in fifteen years?

CHRIS. (*Suddenly growing somber—in a low tone*) No. Ven she vas little gel, Ay vas bo'sun on vindjammer. Ay never gat home only few time dem year. Ay'm fool sailor fallar. My voman—Anna's mother—she gat tired vait all time Sveden for me ven Ay don't never come. She come dis country, bring Anna, dey go out Minnesota, live with her cousins on farm. Den ven her mo'der die ven Ay vas on voyage, Ay tank it's better dem cousins keep Anna. Ay tank it's better Anna live on farm, den she don't know dat ole davil, sea, she don't know fader like me.

2. Later, Chris Christopherson, quite drunk, having sung a sea chantey at the top of his lungs, has this to say:

CHRIS. (*Sitting down*) Ay'm good singer, yes? Ve drink, eh? Skoal! Ay calabrate! (*He drinks.*) Ay calabrate 'cause Anna's coming home. You know, Marthy, Ay never write for her to come, 'cause Ay tank Ay'm no good for her. But all time Ay hope like hell some day she vant for see me and den she come. And dat's vay it happen now, py yiminy! (*His face beaming*) What you tank she look like, Marthy? Ay bet you she's fine, good, strong gel, pooty like hell! Living on farm made her like dat. And Ay bet you some day she marry good, steady land fallar here in East, have home all her own, have kits—and dan Ay'm ole grandfader, py golly! And Ay go visit dem every time Ay gat in port near! (*Bursting with joy*) By yiminy crickens, Ay calabrate dat! (*Shouts*) Bring oder drink, Larry! (*He smashes his fist on the table with a bang.*)

3. In act 3, which is set in the "Cabin of the barge, at dock in Boston," Anna "Christie" Christopherson finally tells her father and Matt Burke about the

life she had led. She clearly has an accent, one lighter than her father's, and substitutes /y/ for /j/, as indicated by O'Neill. Treat this as a monologue, ignoring the interruptions by Chris.

ANNA. (*With a hard laugh*) Decent? Who told you I was? (CHRIS *is sitting with bowed shoulders, his head in his hands. She leans over in exasperation and shakes him violently by the shoulder.*) Don't go to sleep, Old Man! Listen here, I'm talking to you now!
[CHRIS. (*Straightening up and looking about as if he were seeking a way to escape—with frightened foreboding in his voice*) Ay don't vant for hear it. You vas going out of head, Ay tank, Anna.]
ANNA. (*Violently*) Well, living with you is enough to drive anyone off their nut. Your bunk about the farm being so fine! Didn't I write you year after year how rotten it was and what a dirty slave them cousins made of me? What'd you care? Nothing! Not even enough to come out and see me! That crazy bull about wanting to keep me away from the sea don't go down with me! You yust didn't want to be bothered with me! You're like all the rest of 'em!
[CHRIS. (*Feebly*) Anna! It ain't so—]
ANNA. (*Not heeding his interruption—revengefully*) But one thing I never wrote you. It was one of them cousins that you think is such nice people—the youngest son—Paul—that started me wrong. (*Loudly*) It wasn't none of my fault. I hated him worse 'n hell and he knew it. But he was big and strong—(*Pointing to Burke*)—like you!
[. . .]
ANNA. (*To him—seeming not to have heard their interruptions*) That was why I run away from the farm. That was what made me get a yob as nurse girl in St. Paul. (*With a hard, mocking laugh*) And you think that was a nice yob for a girl, too, don't you? (*Sarcastically*) With all them nice inland fellers yust looking for a chance to marry me, I s'pose. Marry me? What a chance! They wasn't looking for marrying. (*As* BURKE *lets a groan of fury escape him—desperately*)

I'm owning up to everything fair and square. I was caged in, I tell you—yust like in yail—taking care of other people's kids—listening to 'em bawling and crying day and night—when I wanted to be out—and I was lonesome—lonesome as hell! (*With a sudden weariness in her voice*) So I give up finally. What was the use? (*She stops and looks at the two men. Both are motionless and silent. CHRIS seems in a stupor of despair, his house of cards fallen about him. BURKE's face is livid with the rage that is eating him up, but he is too stunned and bewildered yet to find a vent for it. The condemnation she feels in their silence goads ANNA into a harsh, strident defiance.*) You don't say nothing—either of you—but I know what you're thinking. You're like all the rest! (*To CHRIS—furiously*) And who's to blame for it, me or you? If you'd even acted like a man—if you'd even been a regular father and had me with you—maybe things would be different!

4. In act 4, Anna has planned to go to New York, but she has yet to leave. The setting is the same cabin as in act 3.

ANNA. (*Faintly*) Come in. (*Then summoning her courage—more resolutely*) Come in. (*The door is opened and CHRIS appears in the doorway. He is in a very bleary, bedraggled condition, suffering from the after effects of his drunk. A tin pail full of foaming beer is in his hand. He comes forward, his eyes avoiding ANNA's. He mutters stupidly.*) It's foggy. (*Looking him over with contempt*) So you come back at last, did you? You're a fine looking sight! (*Then jeeringly*) I thought you'd beaten it for good on account of the disgrace I'd brought on you.
CHRIS. (*Wincing—faintly*) Don't say dat, Anna, please! (*He sits in a chair by the table, setting down the can of beer, holding his head in his hands.*)

ANNA. (*Looks at him with a certain sympathy*) What's the trouble?
Feeling sick?

CHRIS. (*Dully*) Inside my head feel sick.

ANNA. Well, what d'you expect after being soused for two days?
(*Resentfully*) It serves you right. A fine thing—you leaving me
alone on this barge all that time!

CHRIS. (*Humbly*) Ay'm sorry, Anna.

ANNA. (*Scornfully*) Sorry!

CHRIS. But Ay'm not sick inside head vay you mean. Ay'm sick
from tank too much about you, about me.

8
Yiddish Accents

Yiddish, an Indo-European language of the Germanic family, evolved from the Medieval High German spoken by Jews who lived in the lands along the Rhine. It was brought to Eastern Europe in the Middle Ages when large numbers of Jews fleeing persecution settled there. By the eighteenth century, Yiddish had almost disappeared in Western Europe, but it continued to co-exist in Eastern Europe with Polish, Russian, Ukrainian, Hungarian, Romanian, and other majority languages.

Yiddish was the first language of most Eastern European Jews before World War II, and of a vast number of Jewish immigrants to the United States and Western Europe at the end of the nineteenth and the beginning of the twentieth centuries. With the murder of millions of Yiddish speakers by the Nazi extermination machine, it appeared that the language was also doomed. But Yiddish has proved very resilient: Several million people still speak it as a first language, including many Hasidim (ultra-Orthodox Jews), whether they live in New York, London, Paris, or Jerusalem.

Among the many Yiddish dialects that influence the accent in English are the Eastern *Galitzianer* /gah LIHTS ee AH nuhr/ (Galician) dialect, spoken in the region of Galicia, which comprises most of what is now eastern Poland and the western parts of the Ukraine, and the Northern *Litvak* /LIHT vahk/ (Lithuanian) dialect, spoken in northern and western Russia and in Lithuania.

Yiddish (*Idish* /EE dihsh/ in Yiddish), a word that means "Jewish" in the Yiddish language, is written in a modified Hebrew alphabet, and approximately 15 to 20 percent of its vocabulary is derived from the Semitic tongues Aramaic and Hebrew, the languages of Judaism and religious education for millennia. There are also vocabulary elements derived from Slavic and Romance languages. With its colorful idioms, vibrant humor, and earthiness, Yiddish became in the nineteenth and twentieth centuries the vehicle for a brilliant, richly expressive literature, and gave rise to a thriving musical and dramatic theater that also established itself in New York with the massive immigration of Eastern European Jews to the United States.

For an authentic Yiddish accent, listen to Maurice Schwartz as Ezra in *Salome* (1953) and as Dr. Botkin in *Mission to Moscow* (1943), where you will hear his excellent, lightly accented English. He is brilliant in the title role of the 1939 Yiddish-language film *Tevye* /TE vye/, based on stories by Sholem Aleichem; Tevye is a darker character than in the musical *Fiddler on the Roof* (play, 1964; film, 1971). Listen to New York–born Molly Picon (Yente in the film version of *Fiddler*), whose first language was Yiddish, and who was a star of the Yiddish- as well as the English-speaking theater; she co-starred in the film version of Neil Simon's *Come Blow Your Horn* (1963) and in the Yiddish-language film *Yidl mitn Fidl* /YIH dl mihtn FIH dl/ (*Yiddle with His Fiddle*; 1936). Menasha Skulnik, from Warsaw, who was mostly a stage actor, is delightful in his rare television appearances; see him in the semi-documentary *The Golden Age of 2nd Avenue* (1969; reissued in 2009), which also includes footage of Picon, Herschel Bernardi, and the great actor Paul Muni, who also began his career in the Yiddish theater. Skulnik made one episode of the television series *The Goldbergs* (1949–1956), about a Jewish family in New York. The series starred New York–born Gertrude Berg (who also wrote most of the episodes) and featured David Opatoshu (the son of the Yiddish novelist Joseph Opatoshu) and Eli Mintz, from Austrian Galicia. There is also a 1950 film based on the series. Listen to recordings of New Yorker Fanny Brice, with her hilarious Yiddish-accent shtick, and see her in *The Great Ziegfeld* (1936) and *Ziegfeld Follies* (1945). *Hester Street* (1975), written and directed by Joan Micklin Silver and based on a Yiddish novel by Abraham Cahan, gives a detailed picture of turn-of-the-century Lower East Side New York, where many Yiddish-speaking immigrants settled. The film is less authentic than it might be, because the mother tongue of most of the actors was not Yiddish. That said, don't miss the performances of Leib Lensky and Zvee Scooler, who only speak their first language, Yiddish. For a more authentic East European Yiddish *tam* /TAHM/ (flavor; atmosphere), see the DVD of the *Play of the Week*'s 1959 broadcast *The World of Sholom Aleichem*, adapted from the Off-Broadway show, with Zero Mostel (the original Tevye in *Fiddler on the Roof*), Sam Levene, Morris Carnovsky, Jack Gilford, Lee Grant, Nancy Walker, and Gertrude Berg.

Two excellent documentaries are *Yiddish Theater: A Love Story* (2007) and *The Thomashefskys: Music and Memories of a Life in the Yiddish Theater* (2012). And don't miss *The Komediant* /ko me dee AHNT/ (*The Actor*; 1999), a documentary about Pesach Burstein (his first name, pronounced /PE suhkh/, means "Passover"), a Yiddish theater actor / comedian / song-and-dance man, and his family; you will hear Yiddish spoken, and many of the people interviewed in English have Yiddish accents.

Roles requiring Yiddish accents include Abraham Kaplan in Elmer Rice's *Street Scene* (1929), and Libby Hirsch in Leonard Spigelgass's *Dear Me, the Sky Is Falling* (1963). Sarah and Harry Kahn, as well as other characters in the first play of Sir Arnold Wesker's *The Wesker Trilogy*, *Chicken Soup with Barley* (1956), set in a London Jewish milieu, speak with Cockney-influenced Yiddish accents. Many characters in Jerry Bock and Sheldon Harnick's often-revived Broadway musical *Fiddler on the Roof*, based on Sholem Aleichem's *Tevye the Dairyman and His Daughters* and other stories, have Yiddish accents—confined, however, to intonation patterns rather than sound shifts. But Gregory Solomon in Arthur Miller's *The Price* (1968) has a full-blown Yiddish accent.

Teach Yourself Yiddish Accents

1. **Positioning, placement, and use of the muscles of the mouth during speech:** The Yiddish language, and Yiddish accents in English, feel as if they resonate generally just in back of the middle of the mouth. The tongue is down and relaxed. The lips are very slightly protruded, but relaxed. The mouth opening is medium wide much of the time.

2. **The sounds of /r/:** Pronounce post-vocalic (after a vowel) /r/ for a General American Yiddish accent, but drop post-vocalic /r/ for a New York City or London / Cockney Yiddish accent. There are two /r/ sounds:

   a. **The uvular /r/:** The uvular /r/ is usual in most dialects of Yiddish, and carries over into accents in English. For a Galitzianer accent in English, use a uvular /r/. See chapter 2 on French accents for tips on how to pronounce this sound. The Yiddish uvular /r/ is very slightly more forward in the back of the throat than most French versions of the sound.

   b. **The trilled /r/:** Use a trilled /r/ with one tap for a Russian / Litvak accent in English. See the introduction for instruction on how to pronounce the trilled /r/.

3. **Vowels and diphthongs:** The Yiddish vowel and diphthong inventory is the same as in English, with the addition of the intermediate front vowel /ih/, and with the exceptions noted below. Use whichever vowel and diphthong system exists in the surrounding accent native to the English language: There are London / Cockney, New York City, Sydney, and Cape Town Yiddish accents, to cite a few examples.

   a. **The shift from /a/ to /e/:** The sound of the vowel /a/ in *that* does not exist in Yiddish, so /e/ is usually substituted for /a/: *cab* /KEB/, *cap* /KEP/, *had* /HED/, *hat* /HET/, *handle* /HEN duhl/, *magnificent* /ME gnih fih SNT/. But /a/ is often learned, and can be heard as a substitute for /e/ in such words as *revolution* /RA vuh LOOH shuhn/, especially in a Russian Yiddish accent.

b. **The substitution of /aw/ for /oh/:** Substitute the lengthened pure vowel /aw/ for the diphthong /oh/: *go* /GAW/, *home* /HAWM/.

c. **The shift from /o/ to /oy/:** The sound of /o/ does not exist in Yiddish, and the usual substitution is /oy/: *first* /FOYST/, *work* /VOYK/.

d. **The shift from /u/ to /ah/:** There is no /u/ sound in Yiddish, and the usual substitution in an accent in English is /ah/: *but* /BAHT/, *love* /LAHV/.

4. **Other consonants:** The Yiddish inventory of consonants is the same as in English, with the exception of /th / *th*/, which do not exist in Yiddish. And consonants are softer, with less pressure of the tongue on the palate for /d/ or /t/, for instance. The place of articulation of /d/, /t/, /b/, /p/, and /sh/ is slightly forward of the General American position; that is, the tip of the tongue is closer to the upper front teeth.

a. **Devoiced final consonants:** Final consonants in Yiddish are often voiceless, although not always, and this phonetic characteristic carries over into an accent in English: /b/ shifts to /p/, /d/ shifts to /t/, /g/ shifts to /k/: *cab* /KEP/, *end* /ENT/, *had* /HET/, *pig* /PIHK/. Final /z/ usually does not shift to /s/, so *is* (the same verb in Yiddish) is pronounced /IHZ/; a rose is still a /ROHZ/. In final consonant clusters, the last voiced consonant shifts to voiceless: *hold* /HAWLT/.

b. **Adding /g/ to "-ing" endings:** In Yiddish, the sound combination /ihng/ is followed by a distinctly sounded /g/: *singen* /ZIHNG gen/ (to sing). This phonetic characteristic is carried over into an accent in English, so that, for example, *Long Island* is pronounced /LAWNG GI lihnt/ instead of /LAWNG I luhnd/.

c. **The sound of /h/:** There is an initial /h/ sound in Yiddish, so there is no problem doing this accurately in an accent in English. But in a London / Cockney Yiddish accent, drop the initial /h/ sounds.

d. **The sounds of /l/:** There are two /l/ sounds in Yiddish:

1. **The dark /l/:** In the formation of this /l/, the front part of the blade of the tongue is raised so that it almost touches the roof of the mouth behind the gum ridge, but an opening is left. This /l/ is often heard in a Yiddish accent in English. This /l/ resonates where the back vowel /e/ does.

2. **The light /l/:** In the formation of this /l/, the tongue is tensed and its tip pressed against the back of the upper front teeth. It resonates where the front vowel /ih/ does. This /l/ is less often heard in an accent in English.

e. **The sounds of /th / th/:** The consonants /th/ and /th/ do not exist in the Yiddish language. Substitute /d/ and /t/: *this thing* /DIHS TIHNGG/. Between vowels /th/ is sometimes heard as an aspirated tapped /d/: *father* /FAH duh (alternatively, der)/.

f. **The shift from initial semi-vowel /w/ to consonant /v/ and the occasional shift from /v/ to /w/:** The sound of the semi-vowel /w/ at the beginning of a word does not exist in Yiddish, and /v/ is usually substituted for it: *one* /VUN/, *when* /VEN/, *won* /VUN/. When the letter combination "qu" is used in English spelling it is pronounced /kw/, a sound that also does not exist in Yiddish. In a Yiddish accent in English, the sound /kv/ is substituted for /kw/: *queen* /KVEEN/, *quite* /KVIT/.

Often, people learn to pronounce /w/ correctly, especially in a lighter accent, so you don't always have to do the shift from /w/ to /v/.

Occasionally, initial /v/ shifts to /w/ in a very heavy accent: *visit* /WIH ziht/, *invite* /ihn WIT/. But this is by no means always done.

For a light accent, keep the general positioning of the mouth muscles consistent during speech, using the Yiddish position when speaking English. Make the consonants hard, especially final consonants, particularly /d/, /t/, and /ng/.

For a lighter accent, use a retroflex /r/, with the tongue only slightly curled upward. To make the accent heavier, add some of the intonation patterns discussed here.

Intonation and Stress: The Music and Rhythm of the Accents

Stress in Yiddish is random, so stress in English is generally easy for Yiddish speakers. Yiddish and English stress patterns are similar: In both languages, longer sentences are separated into phrases in order to communicate information, and each phrase has its own pitch and stress patterns. These are flexible, but each word nevertheless retains its stress, and the most important word receives the greatest stress.

Occasionally, words in a Yiddish accent in English are incorrectly stressed. For instance, the word *carpenter* might be pronounced /kahr PEN tuhr/ with the second syllable stressed, as it was in a famous "dialect" vaudeville sketch from the 1920s, or *capitalist* pronounced /ke PIH tah lihst/, as it is by Mr. Kaplan in *Street Scene*.

The expressive intonation patterns of a Yiddish accent in English have tremendous melodic variety, and are very distinctive and characteristic, carried over from the Yiddish language, as you will see in the practice exercises. They have often been described as "sing-song" because they hit many more upper and lower notes than do most varieties of Standard English.

Practice Exercises
Practice in Yiddish
Note: These exercises are transliterated from the modified Hebrew alphabet in which Yiddish is written.

1. *Sholem aleikhem. Vos makht ihr? Zayer gut, a dank. Un ihr?* [formal "you"]
/SHO luhm ah LAY khuhm / VOS MAKHT EEuhr / ZAY uhr GOOT ah DAHNK / oon EEuhr/

Literal translation: Peace (be)-with-you. What make you? Very good, a thanks. And you?

Translation: Hello. How are you? Very well, thanks. And you?

2. From Sholem Aleichem's *Funem Yarid: Lebensbeshreybungen* /FOO nuhm yah RIHD LEB ents buh SHRI boong guhn/ (From the Fair: Life Descriptions; 1916), Kapitel 1 /kah PIH tel AYNTS/ (Chapter 1), "Far vos epes funem yarid?" /fahr VOS e pihs FOO nuhm yah RIHD/ (For What [Why] Something "From the Fair"?)

Sholem Aleichem (1859–1916), the pen name for Solomon Naumovich Rabinovich, is considered the greatest of all Yiddish authors and playwrights. His bittersweet stories are full of ironic, wry humor and insight not only into the conditions of life for Jews in his homeland, the Russian part of Galicia (a vast region that crossed borders, so that part of Galicia was a province of the Austro-Hungarian Empire), but also into the circumstances and situations of humanity in general. Here are the opening lines of his semi-autobiographical novel, published in 1916.

> Funem yarid kan hayssen funem leben vos is geglikhen tsu a yarid. Ieder iz a veln dos menshens leben tsu perglikhen, nokh zayn hashenah, nokh tsu epes a zakh. Lemshl, eyner a stolir, hat amol gezogt: der mensh iz geglikhen tsu a stolir; a stolir lebt un lebt, dernokh shtarbt er, azoy iz a mensh a zakh . . .

/FOO nuhm yah RIHD kahn HAY suhn FOO nuhm LE buhn vos *IHZ* ge *GLIH* khen tsooh ah yah RIHD / YE der *ihz* ah VELN dos MEN shuhnts LE buhn tsooh per *GLIH* khen / nokh zIn HAH she ne / nokh tsooh E pihs ah ZAKH / LEM shl AY ne rah STAW *lihr* hot ah MOL ge ZOKT / der MENTSH *ihz* ge GLIHKH uhn tsooh ah STAW *lihr* / ah STAW *lihr* LAYPT oon LAYPT / der NOKH SHTAHRPT er / ah ZOY *ihz* ah MENTSH ah ZAKH/

Literal translation: "From the Fair" can be called "About the Life What Is Compared [That Is Comparable] to a Fair." To-everyone is [Everyone has] a wish man's life to compare, either to his [own] year[s] [life], or to something a thing [something else]. Lemshl, one a cabinet-maker, has a-time [once] said, "The man [Man] is comparable to a cabinet-maker; a cabinet-maker lives and lives, thereafter [then] he dies, thus is a man a thing . . ."

Practice in English

3. *I told him, "Don't do it!" But did he listen? No! That's him!*
/I TAWL dihm dawn DOOH iht / baw DIH dee LEES ihn / NOH / dahts HIHM/

```
                                        No!
    told                                        hi-\
        him,        it!"                         m!
 I          "Don't      But       ten?
                do        did he
                        lis-            That's
```

4. *What do you want from my life? Because you forgot it's my fault?*
/VAH duh yuh VAHNT fruhm mI LIF / BIH kawz YOOH fah GAH dihts MI FAWLT/

```
              want                                  ult?
                                          got
What do you
              from my                 for-
                  life? Be-      you
                        cause           it's
                                        my
                                        fa-
```

Note: The /d/ sounds in the syllables /duh/ and /dihts/ are tapped.

Two Scenes and Two Monologues

1. From Elmer Rice's *Street Scene* (1929), Act 1

It is the sweltering hot summer of 1929, just before the stock market crash on Wall Street, which led to a worldwide depression. On a street in front of a walk-up apartment house in "a mean quarter of New York," the people who live in the building are outside to escape the oppressive heat. We see representative immigrants of the period, as well as native New Yorkers.

Sitting at his open window, Abraham Kaplan, a Jewish immigrant from Russia and a socialist, is reading his newspaper and disputing with his neighbors: the Swedish janitor Mr. Olsen, native New Yorkers Mr. and Mrs. Jones, the German-born Mrs. Fiorentino, whose husband is an Italian immigrant music teacher, and the Irish-American Mr. Maurrant. The accents are clearly indicated by Rice.

> KAPLAN. (*Impatiently*) Oll dese unions eccomplish notting wote-ver. Oll dis does not toch de fondamental problem. So long as de tuls of industry are in de hands of de ke*pit*alist klesses, ve vill hev exploitation and sloms and—
>
> MAURRANT. T' hell wit' all dat hooey! I'm makin' a good livin' an' I'm not doin' any kickin'.
>
> OLSEN. (*Removing his pipe from his mouth*) Ve got prosperity, dis coontry.
>
> JONES. You said somethin'!
>
> KAPLAN. Sure, for de reech is planty prosperity! Mister Morgan rides in his yacht and upstairs de toin [they turn] a voman vit' two children in de street.
>
> MAURRANT. And if you was to elect a Socialist president tomorra, it would be the same thing.
>
> MRS. FIORENTINO. Yes, dot's right, Mr. Maurrant.
>
> JONES. You're right!

KAPLAN. Who's toking about electing presidents? Ve must put de tuls of industry in de hends of de vorking [/VOY kihng/] klesses and dis ken be accomplished only by a sushal revolution!

2. Two Excerpts from Leonard Spigelgass's *Dear Me, the Sky Is Falling* (1963), based on a story by Gertrude Berg and James Yaffe

A. In act 1, scene 2, Libby Hirsch, created by Gertrude Berg, is a solicitous mother, talking on the telephone and making plans for her daughter Debbie's wedding. Robert is Debbie's fiancé. Mildred, Libby's sister, is helping out.

Libby's old-fashioned New York City Yiddish accent should be light, mainly heard in hard consonants and intonation patterns. Substitute /oy/ for /o/ in such words as *turtle* /TOY[R] tl/, *sirloin* /SOY[R] loyn/, *dessert* /dih ZOY[R]T/, and *sherbet* /SHOY[R] biht/, with the stressed /oy/ diphthongs heavily r-influenced and spoken with the lips protruded and the tongue held up to the palate.

LIBBY. I'm in a quandary, darling, about the wedding menu. I can't decide whether it should be mock turtle soup or fresh fruit supreme to start. Then, I thought maybe sirloin of beef with potatoes Anna . . . and little French peas . . . and asparagus with hollandaise sauce because Robert loves them. Then a salad—endive—and, for dessert, sherbet and wedding cake. And, of course, wines and salted nuts and peppermints . . . Simple but filling . . . Yeah . . . Uh-huh . . . Are you sure you want to bother with a party for Debbie now? (MILDRED *comes from the dining room with wedding-invitation envelopes.* [. . .]) Did you find the envelopes, Mildred?

B. In act 2, scene 1, Libby has just come home from shopping. Paul, her husband, does whatever she wants him to do. You can treat this as a monologue, with Debbie's line there for continuity.

LIBBY. (*Gaily, as she puts the bag of groceries on the telephone bench*)
What a beautiful summer's day! You know what I just saw? Buds
on the lilac bushes! And you know what that means? It means
summer is just around the corner so we'll give the season a little
push! And tonight we'll have a little cook-out outside. I already
have steaks marinating in soy sauce, and we'll have a salad with
canned asparagus, because Robert loves them—
[DEBBIE. Robert is not coming!]
LIBBY. We'll see. (*Looking at the grocery list*) He only gave me two
cans of asparagus and I ordered three. Well—Paul, darling, take
the cobwebs off the barbecue—get out the cushions for the porch
furniture—and we'll have a regular old-fashioned Sunday-night
supper tonight. Who knows who'll drop in?

3. From Arthur Miller's *The Price* (1968), Act 1

Gregory Solomon is an elderly dealer in old furniture. He has come to
evaluate the contents of a house inherited by two brothers, Victor and
Walter, who do not get along with each other.

Solomon's accent is indicated by the Yiddishized grammar in some of his
sentences, rather than by the sort of phonetic indications given by Rice.
The accent can be light or heavy, as the actor wishes, but his command
of English is good. For a medium to heavy accent, do an occasional initial /v/ substitution for /w/—people can be inconsistent within their own
accents—and pronounce *quicker* as /KVIH kuhr/; elsewhere in this scene,
he pronounces *question* as /KVAS chn/. Solomon would also consistently
substitute /e/ for /a/, as in the words *ask* /ESK/ or *personalities* /POY sih
NE lih tees/. Do an occasional trilled or uvular /r/, and do consistently
the /oy/ substitution for /o/ in such words as *furniture* /FOY nih chuh/,
tuberculosis /tuh BOY kyuh LOH sihs/, and *world* /VOYLT (alternatively,
VOYLD)/. Unlike the r-influenced /oy/ sounds in Libby's accent in the
preceding selection, these /oy/ sounds are not r-influenced and the tongue
is not held up to the palate when pronouncing them.

SOLOMON. Unless we're gonna talk about a few pieces, then it wouldn't bother me, but to take the whole load without a paper is a—

VICTOR. All right, I'll get you some kind of statement from him; don't worry about it.

SOLOMON. That's definite; because even from high-class people you wouldn't believe the shenanigans—lawyers, college professors, television personalities—five hundred dollars they'll pay a lawyer to fight over a bookcase it's worth fifty cents—because you see, everybody wants to be number one, so . . .

VICTOR. I said I'd get you a statement. (*He indicates the room.*) Now, what's the story?

SOLOMON. All right, so I'll tell you the story. (*He looks at the dining-room table and points to it.*) For instance, you mention the dining-room table. That's what they call Spanish Jacobean. Cost maybe twelve, thirteen hundred dollars. I would say 1921, '22. I'm right?

VICTOR. Probably, ya.

SOLOMON. (*He clears his throat.*) I see you're an intelligent man, so before I'll say another word, I ask you to remember—with used furniture you cannot be emotional.

VICTOR. (*He laughs.*) I haven't opened my mouth!

SOLOMON. I mean you're a policeman, I'm a furniture dealer, we both know this world. Anything Spanish Jacobean you'll sell quicker a case of tuberculosis.

SELECTED BIBLIOGRAPHY

Accents Resources

Baldi, Philip. *An Introduction to Indo-European Languages*. Carbondale and Edwardsville: Southern Illinois University Press, 1983.

Barber, Charles. *The English Language: A Historical Introduction*. Edinburgh: The Edinburgh University Press, 1997.

Battye, Adrian, and Marie-Anne Hintze. *The French Language Today*. New York: Routledge, 1992.

Benson, Morton. *Dictionary of Russian Personal Names with a Guide to Stress and Morphology*. 2nd edition, revised. Philadelphia: University of Pennsylvania Press, 1967.

Blumenfeld, Robert. *Accents: A Manual for Actors*. Revised and expanded edition. New York: Limelight Editions, 2002.

———. *Teach Yourself Accents—The British Isles: A Handbook for Young Actors and Speakers*. Montclair, NJ: Limelight Editions, 2013.

———. *Teach Yourself Accents—North America: A Handbook for Young Actors and Speakers*. Montclair, NJ: Limelight Editions, 2013.

Campbell, George L. *Compendium of the World's Languages*. New York: Routledge, 1995.

Canfield, D. Lincoln. *Spanish Pronunciation in the Americas*. Chicago: University of Chicago Press, 1981.

Casagrande, Jean. *The Sound System of French*. Washington, DC: Georgetown University Press, 1984.

Castiglione, Pierina Borrani. *Italian Phonetics, Diction and Intonation*. New York: S. F. Vanni, 1957.

Comrie, Bernard, ed. *The World's Major Languages*. New York: Oxford University Press, 1990.

Croghan, Vera. *Teach Yourself Swedish Complete Course Package* (book + 2 CDs). New York: McGraw-Hill, 2005.

Cruttenden, Alan. *Intonation*. New York: Cambridge University Press, 1986.

Crystal, David. *The Cambridge Encyclopedia of Language*. New York: Cambridge University Press, 1987.

De Mauro, Tullio. *Storia linguistica dell'Italia unita*. Rome: Editori Laterza, 1998.

———, and Mario Lodi. *Lingua e dialetti*. Rome: Editori Riuniti, 1993.

Giegerich, Heinz J. *English Phonology*. New York: Cambridge University Press, 1992.

Gimson's Pronunciation of English. 5th edition, revised by Alan Cruttenden. London: Edward Arnold, 1994.

Harris, Martin, and Nigel Vincent, eds. *The Romance Languages*. New York: Oxford University Press, 1988.

Hirst, Daniel, and Albert Di Cristo, eds. *Intonation Systems: A Survey of Twenty Languages*. New York: Cambridge University Press, 1998.

Jones, Daniel. *An English Pronouncing Dictionary*. 15th edition. Edited by Peter Roach and James Hartman. New York: Cambridge University Press, 1997.

Kriwaczek, Paul. *Yiddish Civilization: The Rise and Fall of a Forgotten Nation*. New York: Vintage, 2006.

Ladefoged, Peter. *A Course in Phonetics*. 3rd edition. Philadelphia: Harcourt, Brace College Publishers, 1993.

———, and Ian Maddieson. *The Sounds of the World's Languages*. Oxford: Blackwell Publishers, 1996.

Lepschy, Anna Laura, and Giulio Lepschy. *The Italian Language Today*. 2nd edition. Chicago: Ivan R. Dee, 1998.

Nielsen, Hans Frede. *The Germanic Languages: Origins and Early Dialectical Interrelations*. Tuscaloosa: University of Alabama Press, 1989.

Pei, Mario. *The World's Chief Languages*. New York: S. F. Vanni, 1946.

Pleasants, Jeanne Varney. *Pronunciation of French: Articulation and Intonation*. New York: privately printed, 1964.

Posner, Rebecca. *The Romance Languages*. New York: Cambridge University Press, 1996.

Robinson, Orrin W. *Old English and Its Closest Relatives: A Survey of the Earliest Germanic Languages*. Stanford, CA: Stanford University Press, 1992.

Rosten, Leo, and Lawrence Bush. *The New Joys of Yiddish: Completely Updated*. New York: Three Rivers Press, 2003.

Russ, Charles V. J. *The German Language Today*. New York: Routledge, 1994.

Ryazanova-Clarke, Larissa, and Terence Wade. *The Russian Language Today*. New York: Routledge, 1999.

Skinner, Edith. *Speak with Distinction*. Revised with new material added by Timothy Monich and Lilene Mansell. Edited by Lilene Mansell. New York: Applause, 1990.

Stewart, Miranda. *The Spanish Language Today*. New York: Routledge, 1999.

Sussex, Roland, and Paul Cubberley. *The Slavic Languages*. New York: Cambridge University Press, 2011.

Wells, J. C. *English Intonation: An Introduction*. New York: Cambridge University Press, 2006.

Weinreich, Uriel, and Beatrice Weinreich. *Say It in Yiddish*. New York: Dover, 1958.

Literary Sources

Aleichem, Sholem (Solomon N. Rabinovich). *Funem yarid: Lebensbeshraybungen*. Ulan Press reprint, 2012.

Barrie, J. M. *What Every Woman Knows*. Project Gutenberg electronic edition, 2004.

Blessing, Lee. *A Walk in the Woods*. London: Oberon Books, 1998.

Cervantes Saavedra, Miguel de. *El ingenioso hidalgo Don Quijote de la Mancha*. Project Gutenberg electronic edition, 2010.

Chekhov, Anton. *Dyadya Vanya*. Reprinted in *Sobrannie Sochinyennii v Vosmi Tomakh*, tom 7: *Dramatichyeskie Proizvyedyeniya*. Moscow: Bibliotyeka Otyechestvyennoi Klassiki, 1970.

Coulter, John. *The Trial of Louis Riel*. Ottawa, Canada: Oberon Press, 1969.

Dante Alighieri. *La Divina Commedia*. Edited and annotated by C. H. Grandgent. Vol. 1: *Inferno*. Boston: D. C. Heath, 1909.

Goethe, Johann Wolfgang von. *Die Leiden des jungen Werther*. Project Gutenberg electronic edition, 2011.

Gow, James, and Armand d'Usseau. *Tomorrow the World*. New York: Charles Scribner's Sons, 1943.

Hellman, Lillian. *Watch on the Rhine*. New York: Dramatists Play Service, 1941.

Kaufman, George S., and Moss Hart. *Once in a Lifetime*. In *Three Plays by Kaufman and Hart*. New York: Grove Press, 1980.

———. *You Can't Take It With You*. In *Three Plays by Kaufman and Hart*. New York: Grove Press, 1980.

Latins Anonymous (Luisa Leschin, Armando Molina, Rick Nájera, Diane Rodríguez). *Latins Anonymous*. In *Latins Anonymous: Two Plays*. Houston, TX: Arte Público Press, 1996.

Ludwig, Ken. *Lend Me a Tenor*. In *Lend Me a Tenor and Other Plays*. Hanover, NH: Smith and Kraus, 2010.

Miller, Arthur. *After the Fall*. In *Eight Plays*. Garden City, NY: Nelson Doubleday, 1981.

———. *The Price*. In *Eight Plays*. Garden City, NY: Nelson Doubleday, 1981.

———. *A View from the Bridge*. In *Eight Plays*. Garden City, NY: Nelson Doubleday, 1981.

O'Neill, Eugene. *Anna Christie*. Project Gutenberg electronic edition, 2003.

Proust, Marcel. *Du côté de chez Swann*. Paris: Bernard Grasset, 1913.

Rice, Elmer. *Street Scene*. New York: Samuel French, 1956.

Shakespeare, William. *The Life of King Henry the Fifth*. World Library, Inc./ Project Gutenberg electronic edition, 1997.

———. *Love's Labour's Lost*. World Library, Inc./Project Gutenberg electronic edition, 1997.

———. *The Merry Wives of Windsor*. Project Gutenberg electronic edition, 1998.

———, and John Fletcher. *The Life of Henry the Eighth*. Project Gutenberg electronic edition, 1998.

Shaw, George Bernard. *Man and Superman: A Comedy and a Philosophy*. Project Gutenberg electronic edition, 2006.

Spigelgass, Leonard. *Dear Me, the Sky Is Falling*. New York: Random House, 1963.

Strindberg, August. *Fröken Julie: Ett Naturalistiskt Sorgespel*. Nabu Press reprint, 2012.

Ustinov, Peter. *Romanoff and Juliet*. In *Five Plays*. Boston: Little, Brown, 1965.

Williams, Tennessee. *The Rose Tattoo*. In *Eight Plays*. Garden City, NY: Nelson Doubleday, 1979.

ABOUT THE AUTHOR

Robert Blumenfeld is the author of *Accents: A Manual for Actors* (1998; Revised and Expanded Edition, 2002); *Acting with the Voice: The Art of Recording Books* (2004); *Tools and Techniques for Character Interpretation: A Handbook of Psychology for Actors, Writers, and Directors* (2006); *Using the Stanislavsky System: A Practical Guide to Character Creation and Period Styles* (2008); *Blumenfeld's Dictionary of Acting and Show Business* (2009); *Blumenfeld's Dictionary of Musical Theater: Opera, Operetta, Musical Comedy* (2010); *Stagecraft: Stanislavsky and External Acting Technique—A Companion to Using the Stanislavsky System* (2011); *Teach Yourself Accents—The British Isles: A Handbook for Young Actors and Speakers* (2013); *Teach Yourself Accents—North America: A Handbook for Young Actors and Speakers* (2013); and the collaborator with noted teacher, acting coach, and actress Alice Spivak on the writing of her book *How to Rehearse When There Is No Rehearsal: Acting and the Media* (2007)—all published by Limelight. He lives and works as an actor, dialect coach and writer in New York City, and is a longtime member of AEA and SAG-AFTRA. He has worked in numerous regional and New York theaters, as well as in television and independent films. For ACT Seattle he played the title role in Ronald Harwood's *The Dresser*, and he has performed many roles in plays by Shakespeare and Chekhov, as well as doing an Off-Broadway season of six Gilbert and Sullivan comic operas for Dorothy Raedler's American Savoyards (under the name Robert Fields), for which he played the Lord Chancellor in *Iolanthe* and other patter-song roles. In 1994, he performed in Michael John LaChiusa's musical *The Petrified Prince*, directed by Harold Prince at the New York Shakespeare Festival's Public Theater. For the McCarter Theatre in Princeton, NJ, Robert performed the role of the First Voice in Dylan Thomas's *Under Milk Wood*.

He created the roles of the Marquis of Queensberry and two prosecuting attorneys in Moisés Kaufman's Off-Broadway hit play *Gross Indecency: The Three Trials of Oscar Wilde*, and was also the production's dialect coach, a job that he did as well for the Broadway musicals *Saturday Night Fever* and *The Scarlet Pimpernel* (third version and national tour) and for the New York workshop of David Henry Hwang's rewritten version of Rodgers and Hammerstein's *Flower Drum Song*. At the Manhattan School of Music, he was dialect coach for Dona D. Vaughn's production of Strauss's *Die Fledermaus* (2009) and for Jay Lesenger's production of Weill's *Street Scene* (2008), which he also coached for Mr. Lesenger at the Chautauqua Opera. Mr. Blumenfeld currently records books for Audible. He has recorded more than 320 Talking Books for the American Foundation for the Blind, including the complete Sherlock Holmes canon (four novels and fifty-six short stories), Victor Hugo's *The Hunchback of Notre-Dame*, Alexandre Dumas's *The Count of Monte Cristo*, a bilingual edition of Rainer Maria Rilke's previously unpublished poetry, and a bilingual edition of Samuel Beckett's *Waiting for Godot*, which he recorded in Beckett's original French and the playwright's own English translation. He received the 1997 Canadian National Institute for the Blind's Torgi Award for the Talking Book of the Year in the Fiction category, for his recording of Pat Conroy's *Beach Music*; and the 1999 Alexander Scourby Talking Book Narrator of the Year Award in the Fiction category.

He holds a B.A. in French from Rutgers University and an M.A. from Columbia University in French Language and Literature. Mr. Blumenfeld speaks French, German, and Italian fluently, and has smatterings of Russian, Spanish, Swedish, and Yiddish.

CD TRACK LISTING

Tracks 2 through 8 contain the Practice Exercises of chapters 2 through 8. Track 3 begins with an example from "Intonation and Stress: The Music and Rhythm of the Accents" on p. 49. Track 7 begins with an adapted portion of "Intonation and Stress" relating to Accents One and Two in Swedish (pp. 107–108).

1. List of Phonetic Symbols Used in This Book (4:49)
2. Chapter 2: French Accents (1:15)
3. Chapter 3: German Accents (1:57)
4. Chapter 4: Italian Accents (1:25)
5. Chapter 5: Russian Accents (1:10)
6. Chapter 6: Spanish Accents (1:03)
7. Chapter 7: Swedish Accents (3:45)
8. Chapter 8: Yiddish Accents (1:08)

OTHER GREAT ACCENT BOOKS
AVAILABLE FROM LIMELIGHT EDITIONS

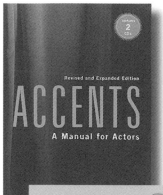

ACCENTS
 A Manual for Actors –
Revised & Expanded Edition
by Robert Blumenfeld

9780879109677 • $29.99 • HL00332412

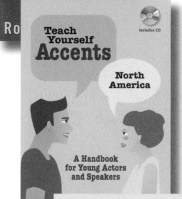

TEACH YOURSELF ACCENTS NORTH AMERICA
 A Handbook for Young Actors
and Speakers
by Robert Blumenfeld

9780879108083 • $19.99 • HL00109569

TEACH YOURSELF ACCENTS THE BRITISH ISLES
A Handbook for Young Actors
and Speakers
by Robert Blumenfeld

9780879108076 • $19.99 • HL00109568